MAKING THE "TERRIBLE" TWOS TERRIFIC!

JOHN ROSEMOND

Andrews McMeel
PUBLISHING®

ACKNOWLEDGMENT AND DEDICATION

As is often the case in the publication—or in this case, re-publication—of a book, the person most deserving of my thanks is Christine Schillig, who not only is my editor at Andrews McMeel but eventually became my in-house "agent" as well. Chris believed in my mission and advocated for me at every possible turn. Therefore, with as much gratitude as I can muster, which isn't near enough, I dedicate this book to her. Long may you run, Chris.

Andrews McMeel Publishing
a division of Andrews McMeel Universal
1130 Walnut Street, Kansas City, Missouri 64106

www.andrewsmcmeel.com

17 18 19 20 MLY 10 9 8 7 6 5

ISBN: 978-1-4494-2160-1

Library of Congress Control Number: 2012954171

CONTENTS

INTRODUCTION

The year between a child's second and third birthdays is the "hump" of parenting. Parents who get over it successfully set positive precedents that ensure smooth sailing from that point on, to the greatest degree possible. That is not to say those parents won't experience future problems. They will, for human beings are the most problematic of domestic species. A high-strung puppy, once properly trained, is never a problem again, but even a very well-trained child is still going to present the occasional difficulty for his or her parents. The difference between the puppy and the child is free will, and free will sometimes leads to perplexing, irritating, and even downright rebellious choices. But parents who have set the right precedents during this critical year will be able to correct these occasional deviations with a proper presentation of love and authority (a major part of which is the ability to remain calm and purposeful in the face of such things).

The third year of life is when—if they are on schedule—parents set about establishing their authority over a child who has been on an all-inclusive entitlement program to that point. It is known as the "terrible twos" because as parents take on this task, the child pushes back with all of his emotional strength, and as anyone who's been in this particular storm can testify, the emotional strength of a toddler can reach hurricane-like intensity. Understandably, the child does not want the entitlements to end. In fact, he demands that they continue in perpetuity, leading to the toddler's reputation for irrational defiance and out-of-control rages when he doesn't get his way.

For two years, he has been led to believe that he is the center of the Universe, the Almighty I Am, and he is not about to relinquish that status without a fight. (Note: The so-called terrible twos can begin as early as eighteen months with some children and can last several months past the third birthday, but the intensity of any child's push-back peaks sometime between birthdays two and three.)

In the face of this tempest, many parents begin stumbling and losing their way. They hesitate, and in hesitating, they lose their authority. In the course of second-guessing themselves, they begin zigging and zagging all over the parenting playing field, trying to figure out how to please their little tyrants. That's the problem right there: trying to please someone who cannot be satisfied. By definition, tyrants are insatiable. Besides, the last time I checked, it's the child's responsibility to please his parents. The parents in question dither, reverse course, give in, blow up, and even give up. In the process of all this zig-zag, they are apt to turn tyrants into full-blown monsters.

I've had a lot of up-close-and-personal experience with toddlers: two of my own, and then the seven they brought into the world. And I've had a lot more second-hand experience in the course of counseling parents of toddlers, helping them get through this all-important phase with as few mental scars as possible. I've put all that experience together in this book. It's designed to serve as a map to guide parents from one side of the minefield to the other. Under the very best circumstances, however, some of the mines will explode. In that event, dust yourself off, collect your wits about you, and keep pushing forward with purpose and as much grace as you can muster.

Keep in mind, always, that you're dealing with a little person who does not know what is in his best interest. He doesn't know what his parents *should* do; he only knows what he *wants* them to do, and most of his wanting is not in his best interest at all. It's what you want for him—the quality of his future—that's of the utmost importance.

What should you want for him? Great question. When I am working with parents in a small group, I have each of them write a ten-word or -phrase description of the adult they want their child to be when he or she is thirty years old. Every parent comes up with essentially the same description: responsible, hard working, honest, ethical, compassionate, charitable, modest, and so on. This is a description of the child's *character,* not achievements. That's the only proper parenting target, I tell them, and one should begin consciously and purposefully aiming at that target when their child is two. From that point on, every single thing you do should be for the single purpose of advancing your child toward that character-based goal. That single-mindedness keeps a parent moving in a straight line from Point A (the young child's second birthday, when his character education begins in earnest) to Point B (the young adult child's successful emancipation from the home). The lack of that single-mindedness, largely due to a lack of clarity about one's mission, causes zig-zag. When storms arise, that determination will make the difference between weathering them and letting them beat you down.

Even the most single-minded parents will make mistakes. In that regard, here are two things to keep in mind. First, being single-minded—staying focused on the adult you want your child to be when he or she is thirty years old—will minimize mistakes and reduce the significance of any one of them. Second—and this is especially the case with a two-year-old—even your parenting decisions that are not the best possible ones will be better decisions than your child would have made for himself. If you are single-minded, that is.

The secret to transforming the twos from terrible into terrific is understanding the nature and course of the child's development during this critical stage, and that:

- The behaviors typically associated with this transition do not warrant overreaction.
- Your role as parent is to bring about a necessary revolution in your child's way of perceiving and relating to you and the world.

- The typical two-year-old is not inclined to cooperate in this revolution.
- A loving yet firm approach to discipline is the means of negotiating these potentially perilous developmental straits.
- You must discipline yourself in order to be effective at disciplining your child.
- Any parental behavior that is driven by fear or frustration lacks discipline; this is the most precedent-setting time in the parent–child relationship.
- You *choose* the precedents that are set.
- If you negotiate the challenges of this all-important developmental stage with grace, skill, and confidence, things will never get this tumultuous again.

I wrote this book to help parents understand the nature of the child at this important stage, become and stay single-minded, get over the hump in question, do what is best for their children when their children want what is not best, and set positive parenting precedents in the process. It was my intent to write a book that is low on theory and high on service, one that is, more than anything else, useful—like a road map. My purpose is to help parents have a happy parenthood and raise happy children whose character shines through everything they do. The twos is where it all begins. It's when true parenting starts.

CHAPTER

1

The Big Picture

If it were possible to record and decode the flurry of activity that occurs in the brain of a newborn child at the moment he first opens his eyes to behold the mysteries of the universe, the translation would probably read, "Wow! Look what I did!" Lacking any other frame of reference, the infant relates all early experience to himself and himself alone. From his point of view, the world came into being at the moment he opened his eyes; therefore, the act of opening his eyes was the Act of Creation. From his point of view, it follows that he reigns supreme over all things, which exist for him and because of him. Amen.

"Egocentric" was the label Swiss developmental psychologist Jean Piaget (1896–1980) used to describe the infant's sense of omnipotent self-centeredness. This belief, that he is the All-Powerful Prime Mover and Shaker, is the child's first construction of reality. And for the first two years or so of his life, his parents and other significant adults—if they are sensitive to his needs—respond to him *as if that belief were true*. When he's hungry, he signals to be fed, and someone feeds him. When he's tired of walking, he signals to be carried, and someone carries him. When he wants attention, he yells, and someone appears, eager to do his bidding. And on and on it goes; whether uncomfortable, frustrated, or just plain bored, he plays the tune and his parents (and other responsible adults) dance. Add to this the fact that as his parents push him through public places in his portable throne, people are constantly approaching and kneeling in front of him, begging for the favor of a smile. Given the manner in which he is treated and responded to during his first two years, he has every reason to believe he is El Magnifico Supremo, The First and Only One of Any Importance over Whose Illustrious Countenance the Sun Rises and Sets. Long before his second birthday, his sense of well-being has come to rest on the conclusion, arrived at honestly, that he rules the world. (He does not yet know that the world is a very big place.)

In the process of catering to his self-centered fantasies, his parents have established one abiding, all-important understanding: Beyond any doubt, he can rely on them. That sense of reliance is known as *trust*. That quality of the early parent–child relationship provides the stability, the ballast the child will need to navigate the occasionally stormy waters of childhood.

Sometime around his second birthday, his parents initiate the most significant transition that will ever take place in their relationship with him. They begin moving from the first to the second of parenthood's seasons. (More on this important subject in a moment.) If this year-long transition is successful, they begin El Magnifico Supremo's transformation into a responsible member of society. They begin refusing to cater to his every whim. They insist that he begin doing certain things for himself. They make him wait for things he wants, and even, on occasion, reject his demands completely and without explanation. In short order, they change the name of the game from "You're in Charge" to "We're in Charge." This effectively yanks the rug of the child's self-centered sense of well-being out from under him, lands him on his regal butt, and makes him completely and ferociously furious. He becomes *Toddlerus terribilius,* a highly dangerous and unpredictable creature prone to biting the very hand that feeds him.

In response to this uprising of the servants, the toddler does what should come as no surprise to anyone: He screams, refuses to cooperate or even negotiate with the leaders of the rebellion, and denies that they have the power to accomplish their aims. They say "sit down"; he stands up. They tell him to pick up his toys; he refuses. If his parents deny him something, he falls on the floor, flailing and screaming incoherently. Such is the price that his parents (and others) must pay to tame the beast within.

Getting Off on the Right Foot

Just as there are seasons to farming and the migrations of fish and birds, there are seasons to the raising of a child, each of which involves distinct parental responsibilities.

In 2010, I spoke on the concept of parenting seasons to an audience at an Orthodox Jewish synagogue in Dallas, Texas. After my talk, the rabbi told me that everything I'd said along those lines was affirmed in the ancient writings of Jewish culture. In fact, there is historical evidence that in many traditional cultures the raising of children was conducted in accord with the intuitive understanding that child rearing is seasonal in nature.

The first of these—I call it the Season of Service—begins at birth and lasts for approximately two years. During this time, parents are servants to a child who cannot serve himself or anticipate the consequences of his own behavior. This state of all-inclusive dependency requires that his parents place him at the center of their attention and orbit around him in a near-constant ministry of vigilance and doing. They must not only provide for his basic needs but also protect him from harm that he might bring on himself in the course of exploring his environment.

In all cultures and in all times, the mother has been and is the primary servant during season one. There are individual exceptions to this (e.g., when the mother dies in childbirth), but there are not and never have been any cultural exceptions. The father, even one who wants to be highly involved, stands slightly outside the periphery of his wife's busy orbit, functioning as her parenting aide. His job is to assist his wife and fill in for her when she needs a break from child-rearing responsibilities. Because the family is child-centered during this first season, the marriage goes to the proverbial back burner. The roles of husband and wife become subordinate to the roles of father and mother. Figure 1 shows a family map of season one.

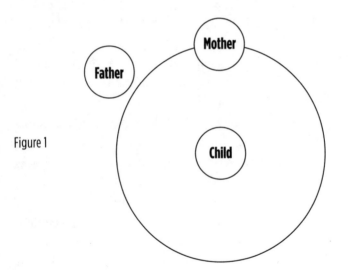

Figure 1

It's important to understand that the infant or young toddler has no appreciation of his dependency. From his perspective, he's running the show. His parents exist to do things for him, make him comfortable, and satisfy his every desire. More specifically, he has every reason to believe that his mother *belongs* to him, that he has power over her. This inarticulate belief is verified every time he emits a loud sound and she appears and sets about relieving his distress. From his point of view, she is well trained but always in need of being reminded that he rules.

When the proper raising of a child was regarded as a fairly practical matter, the purpose of which was to create a good citizen, and not imbued with a confusing cacophony of largely bogus psychological considerations, a mother understood (without reading parenting books) that what she was doing during her child's first two years of life was absolutely essential, but she was slowly creating a monster. After all, he was beginning to act like one. If she did not bring this first season to a close, she was in danger of raising an insufferable child who would eventually conclude that just as she was doing, so the world revolved around him.

A Change of Season

As her child approaches his second birthday, a mother's task becomes that of redefining her role in his life. Over the next year, she undergoes a metamorphosis. She slowly sheds the role of servant and begins to occupy the role of authority figure. Slowly but surely, she leads herself and her child into the next parenting season, the Season of Leadership and Authority. This transitional year is the single most important, precedent-setting time in the parent–child relationship. It determines whether the child's discipline will go smoothly or be a problem-ridden and highly stressful process for all concerned.

By the time her child is three years of age—assuming her single-mindedness—he sees his mother with new eyes. Once a servant, she is now a formidable authority in his life. She has entered season two of parenting. As she underwent this transformation, she slowly took him out of the center of her attention and moved herself into the center of his attention. As your great-grandmother could have told you, there is no magic to this. It is a simple matter of *acting like you know what you are doing*. You are decisive, directive, and steadfastly purposeful. Although you care deeply for your child, you do not care whether he approves of your decisions. You love your child and are confident that you know what is best, and that's the long and short of it.

By the time a child is three, he understands either that (a) it is his job to pay attention to his parents and do what they tell him to do, or (b) it is their job to pay attention to and do things for him. It is essential that the child reach conclusion (a) to ensure his proper discipline from that time forward. The root word of *discipline* is *disciple,* or student. Quite obviously, one cannot effectively teach if the student is not paying attention, and the equally simple fact is that *the more attention a parent pays a child, the less attention the child will pay the parent* (and the more attention he will demand).

The Stumbling Block of Parent-Babble

Moving from season one to season two was not problematic for a mother in the 1950s and before. But then those moms were not consuming advice from professional parenting experts. They were simply doing what came naturally, what their foremothers had done for many prior generations. Modern parenting propagandists—and by that I mean at least 90 percent of people who write on the subject—have caused today's typical mom to believe that the best mothers pay their children as much attention as possible. That's certainly true (within limits) during season one, but the requirements of that first phase of child rearing are unique. What is functional to those first two years is not functional to any other parenting season.

Today's moms probably pay ten times more one-on-one attention than mothers in the 1950s and before paid to their kids. Pre-1960s moms supervised their children well but didn't accord them a great deal of one-on-one "mommy time" (take it from someone who was raised back then). She was available, and mother–child interactions were occasional, but by the time her children were three years of age, the traditional mother expected them to entertain themselves, do their own homework, study independently for tests, do their chores without being told, solve social problems that arose at school or with peers, wash and bandage their own cuts, and so on. The mother–child relationship was relaxed, as opposed to being driven by lots of anxiety and concern, as is all too often the case today. The change from low-involvement parenting (which promotes independence) to high-involvement parenting (which involves a lot of enabling and promotes dependency) occurred because of babble from parenting experts such as psychologist Thomas Gordon, the author of the best-selling parenting book of the early 1970s, *Parent Effectiveness Training*.

Gordon insisted that the only healthy family was a child-centered family—not just during season one, mind you, but in perpetuity. He maintained that this state of affairs was essential to child mental health and the acquisition of high self-esteem, which was a brand-new concept at that time. American parents, not knowing that ever since Freud, psychologists have been making things up and passing off one ill-researched fiction after another on an unsuspecting public, believed Gordon knew what he was talking about. After all, he was a psychologist. The problem was increased by the fact that pretty much the entire mental health community jumped on Gordon's progressive parenting bandwagon. For more on this, see my book *Parent-Babble* (Andrews McMeel, 2012).

It's an indisputable fact that mothers are the primary consumers of parenting information. Thus, moms became convinced that proper parenting was largely a matter of paying children as much attention as possible, praising them often, interacting with them as much as possible, and doing lots of things for them and with them. Older women could have told them this was hogwash, but mothers were no longer listening to their elders. They were (and still are) listening to the likes of Gordon. In effect, he was promising a parenting utopia, an idyllic parent–child relationship that was devoid of difficulty because in his alternative universe, parents and children were equals and the family was a democracy. Gordon's sales pitch worked to transform America's parenting culture and families. Unfortunately, his promises didn't pan out. They backfired, which explains why today's children are so much more problematic than kids raised before professionals like Gordon began marketing a radically new parenting paradigm. High-involvement parenting may sound all warm and fuzzy, but because it is perpetually child-centered it effectively prevents a child from understanding that it's his job, from age three on, to pay attention to his parents. Long past his third birthday, he experiences his parents still acting as if season one is never-ending. As a consequence, he is far more difficult to discipline than was a child in the 1950s and before. Not surprisingly, his parents have major problems even getting his attention, not to mention getting him to do what they want him to do.

My overarching purpose in writing this book is to help parents—more specifically, mothers—avoid this contemporary pitfall and make the transition from season one to season two successfully. To do so, today's mother must be willing to parent against the grain. The style of parenting that I'm going to describe is not the norm today. Ironically, it was the norm before the psychological parenting revolution that took America by storm in the late 1960s and early 1970s. Today, adopting this parenting style requires not only that a mother be unaffected by what her child thinks of her decisions but that she also be unaffected by what her peer group thinks of how she is raising her child. This is not easy, but the right thing is often not the popular thing. It's often the more difficult road to travel. But in this case, it is the more rewarding road, believe me.

The Road Less Traveled, or How to Become a Part-Time Mom

Now, let's get back to accomplishing this all-important transition, the mother's metamorphosis, and setting the child's future discipline on the proper course. But first, I should explain why I'm talking almost exclusively about mothers. Aren't fathers important? Yes, they are. All the research finds that loving fathers make a huge positive difference in every aspect of their children's lives, from school performance to peer relations. But because the mother is the front-line parent during season one, because she is performing most of the parenting responsibilities during that time, the most pressing issue is her child's perception of *her*. It might be more "correct" if I held fathers and mothers equally responsible for the success of this seasonal transition, but the fact is that the mother must initiate this revolution of understanding in her child's life, and she must see it through. She needs her husband's steadfast backing, of course, but in the final analysis, the success of this year-long transition is up to her. By no means am I loading yet another parenting burden on the shoulders of mothers. In fact, I'm going to describe how a mother can prevent parenting from ever becoming burdensome. Here goes. There are three things a mother must do in order to move herself into season two, even if she must drag her child kicking and screaming behind her.

The First Thing
Mom must significantly lower her level of doing for her child. One at a time, she must assign to her child responsibilities she has been performing on his behalf. The mother of several generations past began with assigning her child responsibility for disposing properly

of his own body wastes. Yes, believe it or not, she toilet-trained her child before he was two years old, and yes, it can still be done! I'll describe how in the upcoming chapter on toilet training.

Along with teaching her child to use the toilet, mom teaches him to get his own water (before junk-food drinks, water was what children drank between meals, when they drank milk), get basic between-meal snacks for himself, dress himself, and put himself to bed, after which she and his father tuck him in. She delegates responsibility, one of the primary characteristics of good leadership, and remember, she is moving into the Season of Leadership and Authority. In this manner, she not only promotes her child's independence but also becomes, slowly but surely, a part-time mother. How glorious!

The idea that mothering is a part-time job from the third birthday on is revolutionary for today's moms, who have been led to believe that Truly Good Mommies are full-time. Why, the Truly Good Mommy would be on the job 24/7 if she could stay awake. Keep in mind that until the late 1960s, moms felt quite the opposite. They believed that they should do as *little* for their children as possible. That's what my mother thought, to my inestimable benefit. Also keep in mind that those old-fashioned but very commonsensical moms weren't trying to build self-esteem. They were trying to teach their children to stand on their own two feet. Let's face it, when all is said and done, standing on one's own two feet is the key to a happy life. Also keep in mind that the mental health of kids in the 1950s was a whole lot better than the mental health of today's kids. This book will help the modern mom think the same way her great-grandmother thought and experience the inestimable joys of part-time motherhood.

The Second Thing

Mom must begin enforcing a boundary—both physical and emotional—between herself and her child. She begins to limit her child's access to her. She insists that he not interrupt unnecessarily when she is involved in her tasks. She expects him to entertain himself for most of the day and directs him to solve his own problems, whatever they are, although she and his father are still there to solve for him those problems that he simply cannot solve for himself.

In this fashion, Mom further promotes her child's independence (the key to a happy life, remember) and his respect for her. The simple fact is that when there is no boundary in a relationship, one party is free to exploit and take the other party for granted. Simply stated, that describes *disrespect*. I long ago lost count of the number of mothers who have told me they think their children don't respect them. They describe demanding, petulant, ungrateful children who seem to feel that having their mothers at their beck and call is a never-ending entitlement. They won't even let Mom talk on the phone without interruption.

The lack of boundary in today's mother–child relationship is ubiquitous. But it's certainly understandable, given the plethora of parenting advice to the effect that the Truly Good Mommy drops what she is doing and pays attention to her child whenever he wants something from her. I once came across an issue of a popular parenting magazine on the cover of which was emblazoned "Ten Things You Should NEVER Say to Your Child." The ten verboten things included "I don't have time for you right now," "I don't really care how you feel about that," "You're going to have to do that without my help," and "You're bothering me; leave me alone." According to the author, each of these brought on psychological confusion and trauma of some apocalyptic sort. Funny, my mother said these things to me and I managed, somehow, to reach adulthood with no more than the normal complement of quirks. This article is an example of how parenting propaganda denies moms the right to enforce boundaries between themselves and their kids, to have lives outside of being mothers. Propaganda of this sort exposes mothers to exploitation, demand, and ungratefulness on the part of their kids. Unfortunately, unmitigated junk of this sort is the norm in today's parenting literature. And remember, it is the rare dad who reads parenting magazines. This junk does brain damage to women.

The Third Thing

Mom (with Dad's eager help, of course) reinstates the marriage as the primary, central relationship in the family. As she transforms herself from servant to authority figure, she transforms herself back into a wife first and a mother second. Simultaneously, her parenting aide does likewise; he becomes a husband first and a father second. These now happily "remarried" people begin paying more attention to each other than they pay their child. They talk more to each other than they talk to him. They have a weekly date night and take child-free vacations. They make parenting decisions in consultation with each other. Their bed is the marital bed, not the family bed. They have become part-time parents. At the same time, they have become full-time husband and wife. And that is the best news in their child's life.

Here's an indisputable fact: Nothing puts a more solid foundation of security and well-being under a child's feet than the knowledge his parents are in a committed relationship with one another. This is not to say that the relationship is perfect. It's not. No marriage is without blemish. But blemishes aside, the two people in question are committed to their marriage. Nor is this to say that single parents cannot do a good job. My mother was a single parent during most of the first seven years of my life, and she was quite adequate to the task. Nonetheless, all the research finds that children fare better in every regard when they are raised by both a mom and a dad who live under the same roof and are married for the long haul.

A Big Step for All Concerned

By completing this metamorphosis and becoming a unified team, the parents usher themselves and their child into parenting's second season, the Season of Leadership and Authority. Figure 2 shows a family map of this second major stage in the parent–child relationship. The child has been removed from the center of his parents' attention. He is now orbiting around them. They are the sun; he is a planet. They are the focus of his attention. And because he is paying attention to them and they are acting like authority figures, he does what he is told (with occasional deviations), and his discipline proceeds naturally from there.

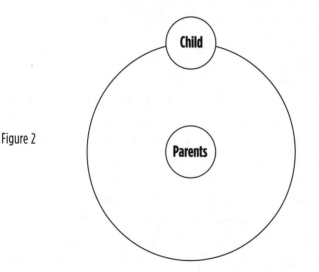

Figure 2

This transitional year is marked by storms of protest from a child who wants season one to go on forever. Who can blame him? Who would not want a servant for life? These storms can be intense and can last for hours. They can be truly terrible. But if the mother stays the course, then by the time her child is three, he will see her as a formidable authority figure. Once he was at the center of her attention; she is now at the center of his. She insists that he do more and more things for himself, that he give her space to do what she needs and wants to do, including putting her feet up and doing nothing, and she makes it perfectly clear that her relationship with his father trumps her relationship with him.

And so begins the Season of Leadership and Authority, during which time the parents' job is to govern the child such that he (1) consents to their government and becomes their willing disciple and (2) internalizes their discipline and gradually develops the self-restraint necessary to govern himself responsibly.

The Final Stretch

Season two lasts for ten years, from three to thirteen, at which point a second transition takes place that moves parent and child into season three, the Season of Mentoring. It is no coincidence that in traditional cultures, early adolescent rites of passage—the Jewish bar mitzvah, for example—occur when a child is thirteen. These rituals mark and celebrate a major transition in the parent–child relationship. They acknowledge that the child in question has completed the disciplinary curriculum of season two and is now regarded as self-governing. He no longer needs adults to tell him what and what not to do; rather, he needs adult mentors to help him acquire the practical skills he will need to emancipate successfully—how to apply for a job, balance a budget, plan for the future, and the like. Figure 3 shows a family map of season three.

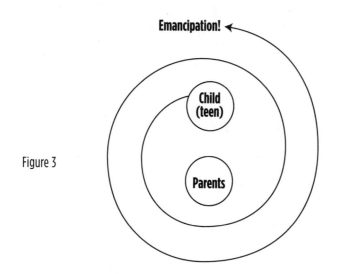

Figure 3

By making the transition between seasons one and two on time and successfully, you guarantee, to the greatest degree possible, that season three will go smoothly. The fact that so many of today's young teens are rebellious, petulant, moody, disrespectful, and lacking motivation is, I'm convinced, due largely to the fact that parents are getting stuck in season one. The mother remains a perpetual servant; therefore, the father remains a perpetual parenting aide. He compensates for the loss of relationship with his wife by adopting the new and very dysfunctional ideal in American fathering: He tries to be his child's best buddy. As a consequence, many an American child is being raised by a servant and a buddy during season two. Needless to say, neither a servant nor a buddy can discipline effectively. And so the child reaches his teen years completely unprepared for the responsibility that goes with the greatly increased degree of freedom he acquires. He begins acting out his unpreparedness in counterproductive and even self-destructive ways.

The new myth is that teen rebellion, petulance, and so on are caused by changes taking place in the young adolescent's brain; therefore, they are inevitable. This is pure hogwash, a form of culture-wide denial. It may be comforting to the parents of an irresponsible, defiant teen who wants nothing to do with his family to think that their child's behavior has nothing to do with them, but historical evidence and American teens who don't fit this negative description prove beyond a shadow of doubt that this sort of behavior is by no means inevitable. It is the consequence not of changes taking place in the brain but of a lack of proper discipline before the teen years. It is the proverbial pigeons coming home to roost.

The bad news is that too many American children reach their teen years still acting like toddlers: tantrums, defiance, petulance, moodiness. The good news is that by reading this book, you are planning ahead in the best way possible. Ironically, the key to successful parenthood during the teen years lies between a child's second and third birthdays. An ounce of parenting prevention is worth far more than a pound of cure.

The Seasons of Parenthood

Season	Age of Child	Parent Role	Parenting Goal
Service	Birth–2	Servant	Secure child
Leadership	3–13	Authority	Self-governing child
Mentoring	13–18	Mentor	Emancipated child

Backtracking

When I'm talking about this critical transition to an audience, the question most frequently asked is, "If my child is older than three, and I'm still acting like we're all in season one, can I recover, or is it too late?"

No, it's not too late. In fact, recovery with a child older than three generally takes less than a year—three to six months, usually.

That's no reason to delay this transition, however, because the emotional toll of waiting more than outweighs the small benefit.

In late 2012, I met a woman who had been dangerously close to mother-madness but managed to recover and tell the tale. She began having children in her mid-twenties. Being well-educated and living in an upper-middle-class urban environment, she was prone to buy into the New Good Mommy Myth, and buy in she did—hook, line, and sinker (with emphasis on *sinker*). After all, it was the norm in her peer group. Her children, eventually numbering three, became her life. Her marriage became an afterthought. In fact, she treated her husband as if he had no sense and couldn't be trusted to ever do the right thing where the kids were concerned. She directed him in his role as father and constantly interfered with any attempt on his part to discipline. A typical story, one I'd heard countless times. From her point of view, he didn't deal with the kids with enough appreciation for their feelings. In fact, when he disciplined them, he sometimes made them feel bad (which is, after all, the point). On the other hand, she disciplined with great compassion, understanding, and sensitivity toward their fragile psyches, which is to say she didn't really discipline at all. She pleaded, encouraged, cajoled, and attempted to reason with her home-grown terrorists.

Eventually, her kids were completely out of control. The school was suggesting that one of them had a serious neurobehavioral disorder. She told me he exhibited characteristics of childhood bipolar disorder, oppositional defiant disorder, and attention deficit disorder. Their pediatrician was recommending medication for him. In all, her kids paid no attention to her whatsoever. The sibling conflict was constant. The house was in constant chaos. She described standing in the middle of the living room, trying unsuccessfully to get her children's attention and then suddenly beginning to jump up and down, screaming like a madwoman. The kids thought it was funny.

One day, she heard Dennis Prager interview me on his syndicated radio show. She went out and bought my book *The Well-Behaved*

Child (Thomas Nelson, 2011), which Dennis had graciously promoted during the interview, read it, and completely transformed her family life in less than six months. Today, her kids are respectful, obedient, and mannerly. The home is peaceful. The marriage is restored. Her friends ask her for parenting advice, so she is now going through training to become one of my Leadership Parenting coaches (for more information, go to my Web site at www.rosemond.com).

She is an example of a woman who became trapped, as do so many mothers these days, in season one but was able to extricate herself and become a formidable authority figure in her children's eyes simply by doing what comes naturally. That's right. Traditional, old-fashioned parenting comes naturally. The new stuff most definitely does not. If the new parenting stuff were natural, it would not result in such anxiety and stress for women.

Questions?

Q *We now realize we failed to accomplish certain goals with our daughter during her twos. Namely, we perpetuated the myth that she was the single most important person in the family. As a result, she is clearly in charge at age four. Is it too late?*

A No, it isn't too late. It is more difficult and more stressful for all concerned to paddle back upstream, but it's not impossible. Furthermore, it is absolutely necessary that you do so, and the longer you wait, the more difficult and stressful it's going to be. Here's how:

- Begin paying more attention to each other than you pay to your daughter. Be husband and wife first, mother and father second. Stop including your daughter in everything you do. Let her know that the marriage is not a threesome.

- Act like authority figures. Remember that authority is an attitude, not a collection of disciplinary methods. Consequences are important indeed, but without the proper parental attitude, no consequence is going to work for long.
- Get your daughter off "family welfare." Assign her a daily routine of chores around the home. In addition to picking up her things and keeping her room neat and clean, you can reasonably expect her to do such things as set and clear the table, help you load the dishwasher, mop hardwood and linoleum floors, dust furniture, and even run the vacuum in open areas of the home. Post the routine on the refrigerator, representing each chore with a picture. Putting her in a responsible, contributing position in the household is essential if she is to begin divesting herself of self-centeredness.
- Stop indulging her every whim. Learn to say "no," and learn to stand firm in the face of her protests. Remember that the more of a tolerance for frustration she develops, the more successfully self-reliant she will eventually become.
- Don't allow her to interrupt adult conversations (beginning with conversations taking place between the two of you), and stop including her in gatherings that are, in truth, adult gatherings. Create a boundary between her and adults. Stop acting like she's simply a smaller version of one. Likewise, keep a healthy distance from her recreation and peer relationships. In order for the marriage to have a life of its own, your daughter must have a life of her own as well.

Q *My husband and I heard you speak in Hawaii and agreed with much of what you said. However, you lost me with all the emphasis you put on not letting children be the center of attention in the family. After all, they're only children for a short time, and it seems to me that letting them be the center of attention for this brief period in their lives does them no harm* *and helps the development of a positive self-image. So what's the big deal?*

A Although children certainly enjoy being the center of their parents' attention, this seemingly harmless state of indulgence eventually impedes their happiness as adults. It extends their emotional dependency, making it difficult for them to emancipate. This is borne out by the fact that since the early 1970s, when child-centered families were becoming the norm, the average age of successful emancipation has increased dramatically. The center of attention is too cozy, too warm and fuzzy. Who wants to leave?

Letting children be the center of attention in a family:

- Makes it difficult for them discover that happiness is something one makes for oneself, not something someone else makes for you. A child with parents who try to keep him happy for eighteen years isn't likely to know how to keep himself happy from age eighteen on.

- Prolongs their self-centeredness indefinitely, and nothing is quite as unattractive in an adult (or a child, for that matter) as self-centeredness. Furthermore, the self-centered adult can never be self-satisfied because he's always looking for someone else to satisfy him.

- Teaches them that self-worth is a function of how much attention they receive from other people. These children become attention addicts, forever unable to satisfy their need to be in the spotlight.

- Turns the family upside down. The center of a family, for the sake of all concerned, should be strong and stable, a place of security that everyone can rely on. The only people potentially powerful enough to occupy that position of responsibility are adults.

- Greatly increases the chances of disobedience. If you act as if your primary job is paying attention to your children, don't be surprised when they don't pay attention to you or do what you want them to do.

♦ Puts on their small shoulders the notion that since they are in control, everything that goes wrong, and especially conflict between their parents (which is inevitable), is their fault. The flip side of feeling like you're the most important person in your family is feeling like you're the most influential as well. Guilt is the boogeyman that lurks in the background of the child-centered family.

Is all that a big enough deal?

Q *You've said children don't need a lot of attention, that too much is addicting, and that families should be adult-centered. How much attention is too much?*

A There is no way to quantify the difference between giving a necessary amount of attention and giving too much. Suffice it to say, the amount of attention a child needs is high during infancy and early toddlerhood and diminishes significantly and steadily thereafter. Dr. Burton White, a highly respected developmental psychologist and best-selling author of *The First Three Years of Life*, has said the single most significant sign of healthy development in a three-year-old is the child's ability to be self-occupied, without making unnecessary requests for adult attention, for long periods of time (an hour at a minimum, on a regular basis). A three-year-old who has received too much adult attention will continue to demand high levels of it. On the other hand, a three-year-old who has not received enough will probably be depressed. Between these two extremes is the three-year-old who has received just enough attention and has learned to trust his parents without depending excessively on them.

To paraphrase Ecclesiastes 3:1, there's a time for giving attention and a time for expecting it. If you give too much, you'll get too little in return.

Q *My first child, a boy, is fifteen months old. I want to do everything I can to make our relationship a special one from the beginning. Specifically, I'd like to be not only a good dad but a good friend. What advice can you give me on accomplishing this?*

A I'd advise you not even to try, because it can't be done. The attempt will cause more problems than you can now imagine. In the course of raising a child, there's a time for being a parent and a time—a much later time—for being a friend. (Ecclesiastes 3:1 applies here as well.) You can't put the cart before the horse, nor can you put it alongside the horse. In this case, the horse is your authority, and the cart is the potential for authentic friendship between you and your son. This potential will become manifest only if you exercise proper authority when it is due and do not confuse the relationship with an attempt to occupy two roles at once.

In trying to be both friend and parent, you will fail at both. When the exercise of authority causes your child to become unhappy with you, as it often will, you will worry that you are destroying the friendship. As a consequence, you will be unable to take and maintain a firm stance on issues. As your child learns to take advantage of your desire to be his friend, he will learn to manipulate you. In response, your frustration will drive behavior that is decidedly unfriendly. This not only will introduce conflict and confusion into the relationship, but it will also saddle you with an almost constant burden of guilt. Under the circumstances, your child is likely to grow up either resenting you or manipulating you, neither of which forms the basis for an eventual friendship.

In short, the better your authority early on, the better friends you and your son will later be. Put first things first.

Q *My thirty-three-month-old daughter insists that I do every-thing for her. She screams if her father picks her up. She runs away from him if he approaches her or tries to help her with something. She refuses to kiss him, won't let him tuck her in, help with her clothes, or even get her a drink of water. If he looks at her, she says, "Tell Daddy to stop looking at me!" This started about a month ago, and it's gotten progressively worse since. What have we done wrong? What should we do?*

A The difficulty you're having with your daughter is not uncom-mon. The many cases of "father-rejection syndrome" I've seen all share a fairly uniform set of characteristics:

- The problem began when the child was two years old, give or take a few months.
- The parent of preference is always the mother.
- The child is usually the couple's first and therefore not just the center of attention but *very much* the center of their attention.

Because of developmental paradigms learned in graduate school, most child psychologists claim that "father-rejection syndrome" is a form of separation (from the mother) anxiety. I don't think so. I think the more likely explanation was advanced by English historian and moralist Lord Acton in an 1887 letter to a high church official: "Power tends to corrupt, and absolute power corrupts absolutely."

From your daughter's point of view, she possesses power over both parents, but Mom specifically. You have been her primary servant for the past two and a half years, during which time Dad has been somewhat of a shadow figure. He's been hard for her to figure out. She doesn't know what to make of him or how to control him. So she wants the person over whom she thinks she has control—Mom!—to do her bidding. Dad just won't do. He hasn't been fully trained yet.

You obviously believe your daughter's demands reflect some psychological need that remains unfulfilled. As long as you think that, this problem is going to worsen. Your daughter will only become more and more demanding.

Your job is to lift the burden of this responsibility from her small shoulders. Find a quiet time to say something along these lines: "Daughter dear, from now on Mommy is not going to do everything for you. Daddy is going to help you, too. He is going to get you water and put on your coat and help with your bath, [and so on]. If you want to scream when Daddy helps you, that's okay. You can scream and you can roll on the floor and kick and spit, but Daddy is going to help you anyway."

Don't make the talk too long-winded, and don't act as if you're seeking her permission to make this administrative policy change. The purpose is not to win her approval or a guarantee of cooperation but simply to give her fair warning that things are going to be different.

From then on, if she needs a drink of water, the parent in the better position should get the water. If Dad gets it and she refuses to drink it, that's her problem. Dad should leave the water where she can reach it and walk away. If someone has to help her on with her coat and Dad is the more convenient someone to do that, then Dad should do it. If she struggles and screams, Dad should do it anyway (firmly but gently), and Mom must not come to the rescue.

Where kisses are concerned, Daddy should definitely not force his affections on his daughter, but if he's carrying her and it feels natural for him to kiss her, then he should feel no reservations about doing so. He might even turn this into a game of "Steal-a-Kiss." A little humor always helps defuse situations of this sort.

It may take some time, but your daughter will get used to it, and her life will be a whole lot better as a result. So will yours.

Q *In one of your talks that I attended, I heard you say that three-year-olds who demand lots of attention have probably received too much to begin with. You were describing my thirty-four-month-old son. As a result of my excessive "mommying," Bubba follows me around the house all day, wanting me to play with him, read to him, get him this, do that. As soon as I begin to do something for myself, he interrupts. I feel like I have no time to myself, no life outside that of being his mother. How can I undo this?*

A As I pointed out in this chapter, women have been encouraged to buy into the falsehood that the more attention they pay their children, the better mothers they are. Female parents do not have full permission to have lives of their own, to pursue personal or professional goals (which is why working moms tend to feel so much guilt), much less say "no" to their kids and mean it.

You've fallen into what I call the Mommy Trap. In the process of paying so much unnecessary attention to Bubba, you've neglected yourself. If you want to help him become more independent, you must begin controlling his access to you. You must let him know, in no uncertain terms, that you are not at his beck and call.

If you can stand some unhappiness (temporary, I assure you) on his part, here are some tried and proven suggestions:

- Make it easier for him to do certain things on his own. For example, if he frequently asks you for something to drink, put a small easy-pour container of juice or water on a low table every morning and teach him to pour his own. (I prefer water because spills are irrelevant; also, the human body is 60 percent *water*, not sugary juice.)
- Pick three things he frequently wants you to do for him but which he can do for himself. Cut pictures out of magazines to represent each demand and glue them on a piece of

construction paper onto which you also glue a photograph of him. When finished, you have a poster that says, in effect, "Bubba can, and will, do these things on his own." Put the poster on the refrigerator, telling him what it means. Tell him you will no longer do the things represented on the poster anymore because he's a "big boy." From then on, when Bubba asks you for one of the things on the poster, take him over to it and say, "This means you can do that for yourself, remember?"

♦ Set aside thirty minutes every morning and every afternoon for Bubba. When you have the time to play with him or read to him, announce that it's now "Bubba Time!" Set your stove timer to ring in thirty minutes. Tell him that when the bell rings, it means you have to stop and go back to your own work (or reading, or whatever).

Bubba may be initially unhappy with these limits, but if you're firm and consistent, he'll make a quick adjustment.

Promoting Healthy Development

Swiss developmental psychologist Jean Piaget dubbed the first two years of life (approximately) the *sensory-motor period*. By that he meant children at this stage are insatiable collectors of information. They are constantly on the move, harvesting and cataloging sensory data about the environment. Their explorations are random but comprehensive. This age child has no blueprint, just an irresistible urge to know everything there is to know about everything there is.

Throughout his meanderings, the infant absorbs an incredible amount of information without knowing how to use it. Sometime during his second year of life, he realizes he can act on the world to *make things happen*. His guidance systems suddenly switch from automatic to autonomous pilot. Until then, he was an explorer, Christopher Columbus reincarnate, out to discover the New World. Now he becomes an experimenter, a little scientist, intent on finding out how things work.

As the sense of the environment is revealed, the toddler begins interacting with it not just curiously but purposefully, to *solve problems.* This quantum leap heralds the advent of what Piaget called the *pre-operational period,* during which the child begins to acquire, by trial and error, the ability to think in terms of cause and effect and, therefore, *operate* meaningfully on the environment.

Example: A fifteen-month-old, seeing a jar of cookies on the kitchen counter, will reach in vain, fall on his butt, and scream bloody murder until someone comes along to lend a helpful hand. Several months later, that same child, spying the same jar of cookies, will push a chair to the counter, climb up, and get the cookies for himself.

As the child's mind expands, so does his world. In no time he is consumed with excitement, a virtual factory of activity. He is on the go during every waking moment, getting into everything, climbing on counters and bookshelves, climbing out of his crib and car seat, always one step ahead of his parents. One thing is certain: He won't take no for an answer. And why should he, when everything around and inside him is saying "Yes! Yes! Yes!" except his parents, who are constantly repeating "No! No! No!"?

One of the limitations nature has imposed on two-year-olds is a gap between physical and intellectual development, favoring the latter. In other words, their physical skills have yet to catch up with their mental ones. A two-year-old may be able to visualize the solution to a problem but unable to perform the movements necessary to carry it out. For example, it may be perfectly clear to him that a certain shape fits a certain space in a puzzle. Nonetheless, he cannot make his fingers work well enough to maneuver it into place. This frustrating disparity is often expressed in sudden, intense explosions. If someone tries to lend a helpful hand, the child may become all the more enraged. His frustration aside, he would still rather do it himself and fail than watch you succeed. Can you blame him?

Sometime around the middle of his second year, the child realizes, in one sudden, insightful moment, that he's a "Me." This is the flowering of individuality, of self-consciousness. The child sets about the task of defining who "Me" is and establishing clear title to that psychological territory. Much to his dismay, as we've already established in chapter 1, he must eventually accept that his boundaries (therefore, his influence) are not all encompassing. "Me" is not the biggest fish in the sea but one of many.

He must learn that independence does not mean doing as he pleases. Just as it is the child's task at this age to establish autonomy (a clear sense of separateness, of individual identity), his parents' task is that of beginning his discipline, his socialization. This requires setting realistic expectations and communicating and enforcing appropriate limits. As his physical and mental aptitudes expand and his desire to master the environment enlarges, so his parents begin making more and more demands on him. They tell him he must do this, and he mustn't do that; he can't touch this, and he can't have that.

It gradually dawns on him that he can't possess the proverbial cake and eat it too. He cannot be independent and comfortably dependent at the same time. In order to become autonomous, he must give up a like measure of attachment to his parents, and Mommy in particular. Whether it is more advantageous to be independent or dependent is a difficult issue to resolve. As a result, the young toddler is a study in contrasts: clinging and cuddly one minute, demanding and defiant the next. He wants the best of both worlds. Don't we all?

As the preceding discussion suggests, the behaviors associated with the so-called terrible twos can be explained in terms of either developmental events, such as gaining the ability to climb, or psychosocial ones, as in parents' attempts to discipline and socialize. Therefore, it is important to understand that getting into everything, tantrums, refusing to cooperate, and so on, are *normal*. Unfortunately, many parents react to them with harsh punishment. True, limits must be set on the child, but there are ways of doing this that do not compromise the child's ability to expand his understanding of how the world works. True, the child must learn that his parents are running the show, but this can be accomplished without suppressing the child's emerging sense of self. True, he must learn he can't always get what he wants (my thanks to the Rolling Stones for this insight) when he wants it, but this can be accomplished without damage to the child's strong-willed spirit. And by the way, concerning the negative connotation of the term *strong-willed,* I'd like to meet the parent who would pray for a *weak-willed* child. We should all join together in blessing strong-willed children, for they are surely the future movers and shakers of the planet.

Before we go any further, let's take a moment to paint a word picture of two-year-olds in terms of the developmental and psychosocial influences that characterize the age:

- Two-year-olds are consumed with the desire to figure everything out. Therefore, they are highly active and get into everything.

- They have yet to develop a tolerance for frustration. Therefore, when things do not go their way—when people do not successfully read their minds, when they don't get what they want when they want it, when their fingers will not cooperate with their eyes and minds—they are likely to suffer instantaneous cerebral meltdown accompanied by much wailing and thrashing about.

- They're unsocialized. Therefore, when they explode, they do so with no regard for where they are, who might be watching, or who might be in the way.

- Young twos still believe they control their parents. They're also developing a clearer sense of themselves as individuals. Therefore, they steadfastly refuse to cooperate with their parents' instructions.

- Twos have every reason to believe that their parents exist to pay attention to and do things for them; therefore, they pay infuriatingly little attention to their parents. They run away from their parents in stores, ignore their parents' instructions, and other equally exasperating actions.

♦ Verbal and intellectual skills are growing by leaps and bounds. Therefore, two-year-olds ask lots of questions. They are self-centered, so they talk to themselves a lot, and when they talk to other people, they're often in their own little world. What results is an egocentric monologue that makes little sense. If you are the audience to one of these soliloquies, don't worry about understanding what's being said (because you won't) or making any sense yourself. Just nod your head, look interested, and say whatever comes to mind (as in a word association exercise). These "conversations" have no rules and can be fun. For example:

Child: "I have a teddy bear."

Parent: "You're my teddy bear."

Child: "Yeah. I'm a teddy bear."

Parent: "And a munchkin too!"

Child: "My teddy bear is a munchkin too."

Parent: "Is your munchkin tired? Does he need a nap?"

As I suggested, say anything and everything that comes to mind. The purpose is the back-and-forth process, not its content.

♦ As the mind expands, so does the imagination. Older twos invent both imaginary friends and fears of many sorts, and they believe that every invention of their minds is real.

♦ Twos tend to want everything on their terms. When you want to pick them up and give them a cuddle, they push away. When both of your hands are busy with something else, they demand to be picked up and cuddled.

♦ The egocentricity of twos knows no bounds, and they think you should be able to read their minds. They want milk. You bring milk. They scream and knock the milk off the table. They said milk, but they meant orange juice. You apologize and bring orange juice. They knock it off the table. Wrong cup! You bring orange juice in the right cup; meanwhile, they've decided milk doesn't sound so bad after all, and on and on it goes. The good news is they tend to sleep anywhere from twelve to fourteen hours a day. The bad news is some of them hardly sleep at all.

In short, this is the best of times, but it can also be the worst of times.

Milestones

Preferring broader strokes, I do not intend to dwell on the details of your child's development. If your curiosity is piqued by the upcoming summation (and I hope it is), I encourage you to broaden your education by reading the 1995 revision of *The First Three Years of Life* by developmental psychologist Burton L. White.

I will simply point out that human children develop along four dimensions, which we artificially separate for purposes of discussion: social–emotional, physical–motor, cognitive (intellectual), and verbal (linguistic). In reality, each dimension, each developmental system, is inseparable from the other three. If you impede a toddler's physical–motor development by confining him to a playpen for significant periods of time, you will also impair the development of verbal, social–emotional, and cognitive skills. Likewise, a child whose verbal abilities are developing slowly may also exhibit delays in other areas. But not always. Sometimes, a child is slow in talking but has the physical–motor skills of a monkey. That would be a boy, mind you.

You can find several lists of developmental milestones for infants and toddlers on the Internet. I like the one from the University of Michigan's medical school at http://www.med.umich.edu/yourchild/

topics/devmile.htm. Keep in mind that age designations are *averages* of when certain milestones are reached. The average *range* for any given milestone, however, lies three to six months on either side of the mean. For example, most children can kick a ball and run without falling down by twenty-eight months. But if your child is twenty-eight months old and falls on his butt every time he tries to kick a stationary ball or trips and falls on his face every time he tries to run, don't panic. In and of themselves, problems like these are no cause for alarm.

Sometimes skills in one area will surge temporarily ahead, somewhat at the expense of gains in the other three. It's as if the child has a finite amount of developmental energy at his disposal. During a certain period of his toddlerhood, if he assigns the majority of this energy to the cognitive realm, then we'll see lots of progress taking place in problem solving. At the same time, little may be taking place in gross-motor skills. Have patience. At this age, as long as things are up to par in at least one area, slight delays (the operative word being *slight*) in the other three are nothing to fret over. The developmentally at-risk toddler is generally lagging in all four areas simultaneously or has a marked delay in one area and is showing little if any progress.

There is something to be said for not getting hung up on milestones at all because few children pass them all right on schedule. If you don't want your anxiety level raised, don't look at the charts. If you can't contain your curiosity, then look at the charts, but please take them with a grain of salt. Regardless, if you have concerns, you should check them out with your pediatrician or family physician. I should note that pediatricians and family physicians want parents to consult them before making appointments with psychologists or other child specialists. As a psychologist, I couldn't agree with them more. Please, please do yourself, your child, and your pocketbook a big favor by running developmental and behavioral concerns by your child's physician. If the doc feels there may be a problem, he will refer you to the person he feels is most qualified to provide the service and most likely to communicate and work cooperatively with him concerning your child's developmental and behavioral needs.

Bringing Out the Best in Your Child

Barring genetic problems of one sort or another, every human being is programmed for competence from the moment of conception. In order to activate this tremendously rich and varied program, all parents need to do is *provide the growing child with a stimulating environment and a variety of interesting experiences that together will enable the growth of competency behaviors.* I know that's a mouthful, but it's really nothing more than a developmental formula for bringing out the best in a child. Every adult who lives with, teaches, or takes care of children shares that pressing moral responsibility.

Seeing to this obligation is neither difficult nor technologically demanding. If you properly assist the development of competence, your child will become independent more quickly, and it should be self-evident that his ability to occupy his own time creatively will be the greatest of all boons to you. So, wasting no time, here are some dos and don'ts for setting up a home-based competency program. Most of it can be accomplished for next to nothing.

Childproof Your Home
Put well out of reach anything that poses a health hazard to your youngster (e.g., cleaning fluids, bottles of alcohol-based products, knives, medicines) and items that are valuable or irreplaceable (e.g., heirloom ceramics, crystal, old photographs). Childproof as much of the house as possible in order to open it to your child's explorations. However, don't just make your home safe; make it stimulating as well. Put things within your child's reach that will be interesting for him to

handle and taste and take apart. The more opportunities a child has to express curiosity, the more his mind will expand. (See chapter 3, "Creative Discipline," for an expanded discussion of childproofing.)

Minimize the Use of Playpens and Other Restrictive Furniture and Devices

This injunction also applies to cribs, walkers, high chairs, and table seats. Playpens have their pros and cons. Used wisely and sparingly, a playpen can perform a valuable service for parents and provide a toddler with a safe, albeit temporary (please!), place to stay while a parent cooks, talks on the phone, or goes to the bathroom. Keep in mind, however, that "playpen" is a misnomer, because children do not play in them—not for long, anyway. Overused, a playpen can be an obstacle to normal development. When left unattended in playpens for long periods, children become bored, frustrated, and even depressed. The best policy is not to use a playpen for more than a few minutes at a time, no more than three or four times a day. If possible, put the playpen in the room you'll be in and talk to your child while you go about your business. I much prefer gates over playpens because they allow much greater mobility. If you don't want to childproof the entire home, then childproof two or three rooms and use gates to restrict your child to those areas.

Encourage and Promote a Variety of Outdoor Activities

Make sure your child enjoys plenty of outdoor time. Toddlers generally love to play in sand, be pushed in a swing, take walks, or just roam out of doors collecting things. While your child is outside, it's perfectly acceptable for you to do nothing but sit and just watch or read a book as long as you balance these sorts of things with some playful interaction. Remember, whether pushing your tot on a swing, rolling a ball back and forth between you, or wrestling in the grass, it's never too late to have a happy childhood!

Encourage and Promote Indoor Activity

The more time your child spends indoors, the more important it is that you provide opportunities for large-muscle development. If you don't provide a menu of appropriate activities, your naturally active and curious child will no doubt invent some that won't be to your liking (e.g., figuring out how to climb onto the kitchen counter). Indoor slides, indoor climbing apparatuses, and other equipment of this sort stimulate gross-motor development. Since young children love nothing more than bouncing on their beds, you might even consider buying a sturdy box spring, setting it off to one side of your child's room or playroom, and letting him bounce on it to his heart's content.

Encourage and Promote Fine-Motor Development

Fine-motor skills are as important as gross-motor skills. Provide your toddler with plenty of crayons and paper, blocks, and interlocking construction toys such as those from Lego (the toddler line is called Duplo). Show your child how things work, how they come apart, and how to put them back together.

Read to Your Child

A home-based competence program recognizes not only the growing child's need for physical activity but also his need for intellectual and creative stimulation. Reading to your child fits the bill perfectly. Beginning no later than age six months, preschoolers should be read to each and every day. Initially, because your child's attention span is short, these sessions will last no longer than five minutes or so. By age three, you should be reading to your child no less than thirty minutes a day. For more on the importance of and how-to of this enriching activity, I highly recommend *The Read-Aloud Handbook* by Jim Trelease.

Talk to Your Child

As I said before, talk to you child even if the conversation makes no sense. Demonstrate and talk about how things work. Ask simple questions and answer your child's questions with simple, direct answers. Before going into a store or any other public situation, tell your child how you expect him to behave. Use language your child can understand—language that's concrete as opposed to being filled with lots of grown-up abstractions (e.g., instead of telling your child to be good in a store, tell him you want him to hold your hand and ask before touching).

Don't Buy Your Child Too Many Toys

Too many toys smother a child's ability to make choices and be creative. You can help develop your child's imagination and resourcefulness (the ability to do a lot with a little) by not buying him a lot. Where toys are concerned, less is definitely more. The few toys you buy should be ones your child can take apart and put together on his own and that allow for lots of creative, constructive behavior. Crayons, clay, Lincoln Logs, Legos (or Duplos), Bristle Blocks, and large cardboard "bricks" are appropriate.

When parents ask, "How can we know a worthwhile toy from one that's a waste of money?" I answer, "If a toy has been in production since before 1955, it's probably fine." With a handful of notable exceptions, every toy manufactured since then has been nothing more than an attempt to reinvent an already-existing wheel. Remember also that in most cases a toddler would rather play with the box a toy came in than the toy itself. When our son, Eric, was two, his toys consisted of some large cardboard bricks, a toy truck, a couple of stuffed animals, a ball, and a large appliance box I'd made into a playhouse. He could play for hours by himself, proving it's not important how many toys a child has but what he's able to do with them.

Parents often ask my opinion of so-called educational toys and toys advertised to strengthen specific skills. My answer is that children can do without them. Generally speaking, claims that a certain toy was designed to promote such-and-such specific developmental skill are hollow. Essential developmental skills will emerge on their own as long as a child is allowed sufficient opportunity to explore and experiment with a variety of everyday things.

Shut Off the Television

Watching television is a "passivity," not an activity. The watcher is both physically and mentally inactive. According to reliable figures, the average American preschool child is watching more than four hours of television per day. That's one-third of a child's discretionary time—time that otherwise would be spent in meaningful physical and mental activity of the kind that promotes creativity, imagination, and intelligence. Remember our formula for promoting competency behaviors? Consider that television is not an experience that involves the exercise of any competency skill. It therefore lends nothing of value to the life of a growing child. In fact, developmentally speaking, television is a *deprivational experience*, which is why I recommend not exposing a child to much, if any, television until he or she has learned to read and reads well. (More on this topic later in this chapter.)

Play with Your Child

I'm not suggesting that you should become your child's primary playmate, but it's important that you make time for relaxed, playful interactions with your toddler. After all, play is the most important thing young children do. Play promotes the growth of imagination and creativity. Games of "let's pretend," which children begin showing interest in shortly after their second birthdays, help them understand and prepare for adult roles. More sophisticated games, which come later, promote social problem-solving skills and help children develop healthy attitudes toward competition. Play also provides children a safe way of expressing socially unacceptable thoughts and feelings. The list goes on: Play exercises gross- and fine-motor skills, strengthens language development, and stretches attention span. In addition, it bolsters initiative and resourcefulness. Last, but by no means least, because it is fun, play helps children develop a good sense of humor.

Studies show that children who enjoy ample opportunity for play are more independent, resourceful, and tolerant of frustration. When they go to school, they are, by and large, the better readers. They are more curious and imaginative. They have better social skills, are less aggressive, and are better at both winning *and* losing. They like themselves better. All in all, they are more fun to be around, for both adults *and* other children.

Playing with a toddler is as simple as providing a few things to play with (a ball, some blocks, a few toy cars) and letting the child take the lead. Just let yourself be a kid again! Roll the ball back and forth, build a block tower and knock it down, crash your cars together! Laugh! Also, don't forget that too many toys and television both throw a wet blanket over the child's playful inclinations.

A True Tale of Too Many Toys

A couple consulted me about their almost-three-year-old daughter, Amanda: "Amanda doesn't want to let us out of her sight," they said. "She follows us around the house, constantly asks us to play with her, and whines if we can't. Neither of us minds playing with her some, but we don't understand why—with all the toys she has—she can't entertain herself occasionally."

My ears perked up. "How many toys does she have?" I asked.

Amanda's dad spoke up. "She has so many you can't walk into her room without stepping on one. We go to the toy store at least twice a month, maybe more. I suppose we've been guilty of spoiling her."

That was the problem, in a nutshell. Not only did Amanda have too many toys, she had all the wrong kinds. First, the confusion of toys in her life made it all but impossible for her to figure out how to use her time. It presented her with an overwhelming number of choices. Second, the playthings themselves were one-dimensional toys that were of little play value (see page 48 later in this chapter for an explanation of this concept). Instead of toys that could be many things, each of her toys was one thing and one thing only. A toy car was forever a toy car and nothing more.

Paradoxically, Amanda's environment was full of fancy things, but it failed to offer sufficient imaginative stimulation and opportunities for creative play. In short, Amanda was bored, and for good reason. The more toys she received, the more bored she became, and the more she looked to her parents to entertain her.

The first thing I had Amanda's parents do was give about 90 percent of her toys to a children's charity. The remaining 10 percent included soft, cuddly dolls that didn't walk, talk, eat, or wet their pants, small human and animal figures, blocks, and a dollhouse. I helped them rate Amanda's toys according to play value on a scale of one to ten, and they donated those with ratings of less than eight.

Next, Amanda's parents went toy shopping. This time, however, they bought only a few toys that would spark Amanda's imagination and therefore keep her interest. These included toys that were multidimensional, meaning toys that could be taken apart and put together again in a variety of different ways, like large cardboard blocks and Duplos.

Then they set up a toy lending library. See page 49 for more on this very practical way of controlling toy clutter and helping children play creatively at the same time.

To create a household environment that encouraged exploration, Amanda's parents childproofed their home. In addition to creating a safe, stimulating environment, childproofing also meant that Amanda would hear the word "no" far less often. Power struggles would be minimized, making obedience more likely.

Amanda's parents put safety latches on all the kitchen cabinets but one, which became Amanda's cabinet. They stocked this cubbyhole with empty oatmeal boxes, empty spools, old pots and pans, small boxes of all sorts, and other safe household items that might otherwise have been discarded. Amanda could go there at any time and rummage to her heart's content.

Last, but not least, Amanda's parents obtained a large appliance box and converted it into a playhouse. They cut a door and several windows. A small chair went inside, along with a pillow and a few dolls. Just the place for hours of imagination.

A few weeks after they made these changes, Amanda was playing on her own most of the day, making far fewer demands on her parents, and acting, in their words, "bright and happy again." Proving, once again, that less is more.

Two True Tales of Television

Every so often, I get up on my Television-Is-Bad-for-Kids soapbox and attempt the all-but-impossible task of persuading parents that television really *does* rot the brains of children.

I don't mean that literally, of course, but I do mean that regardless of the program, *Sesame Street* and other so-called children's programs (they're actually anti-child) included, it wastes their precious time. And their time is of the essence. Study after study confirms that children have about five or six years to get their acts together, so to speak—to get in touch with and develop the many talents and abilities that constitute nearly every human child's incredibly vast and rich genetic heritage.

It's all there from the moment of conception, waiting for a chance to strut its wondrous stuff. Artistic, athletic, intellectual, musical—you name a talent and almost every kid's got it. And nothing more is needed to release this magic than to provide children with *environments and experiences that enable the exercise of excellence.*

Again, this is nothing more than a formula for bringing forth the best in a child. Put the child of great potential in an environment that is both stimulating and receptive to exploration, one that provides experiences that exercise the child's God-given talents and abilities, add the energy and enthusiasm of childhood, and you've got the makings of excellence. It's not complicated.

The key, of course, is the environment, which is where my tirade against television begins. In the last thirty years, television has become a primary environment for children. They spend more time watching television than they spend doing anything else, even going to school. All this watching must be having a profound effect on their development, and it can't be good because a child watching television is exercising not one—I repeat, *not one*—competency skill. And one look at his blank expression will tell you more than words could ever express that this isn't energy and this isn't enthusiasm. This isn't childhood! It's nothing!

I once said all this to an audience at a church in Charlotte, North Carolina. Several weeks later, I received a letter from one of the parents who'd been in attendance. She wrote, "Although skeptical that you could convince me that watching *Sesame Street* was harmful, I went with an open mind. I was always proud of my two daughters'— ages four and two—ability to sit and watch PBS programs by the hour. I thought that since they had never seen a commercial and only watched 'educational' programs, they would be unscathed. I returned home from your lecture and turned off the television. We haven't seen a program since. What amazes me is how we don't miss it at all, and also how much more time we have available to us. Toys that haven't been touched in nearly a year are now being played with daily. We read more stories together and enjoy our days more since we aren't following the television schedule. Thank you for changing our lives!"

This mother's experience with turning off the television is hardly unique. After hearing me speak on the subject, a Waterloo, Iowa mother and speech therapist decided to see for herself whether my warnings about the effects of watching television held any truth. Here, in her words, is her story:

> *Because of your lecture, we established a no-television policy in our home when our daughter, Rachel, was twenty-five months old. Since then, the only television she's watched consists of video-tapes chosen especially for family viewing. This amounts to one or two animated films per week. Furthermore, we only watch a movie after we've read the book together. We noticed an immediate improvement in Rachel's speech and language skills after the television blackout. At twenty-five months (still watching television), she was finally putting two words together. One month after silencing the television, she'd gone from two-word utterances to singing "Angels Watching Over Me, Lord." Three months later, she was retelling* Cinderella *and other favorite books and using as many as nine words per sentence. Before the blackout, she would sit motionless in front of the tube, eyes glued to the screen. She now engages in amazing amounts of make-believe—pretending to be Cinderella, dropping a slipper while she runs away from the "prince" (our cat), and asking me to pretend with her. I'm now thoroughly convinced of the merits of pulling the plug. Speaking as both a mother and professional, I don't believe Rachel would have developed her present skills if we had continued to allow her to watch television an average of two hours per day, as she had done before.*

I can't stress it enough: Television-watching pacifies the growing child's intellect and imagination and interferes significantly with the development of social, perceptual, motor, and language and communication skills. This is true regardless of the program being watched and is why controversy over the content of certain so-called children's programs is nothing more than a red herring. The observation that children show significant developmental gains once television is drastically cut back in their lives is universal. I invite you to prove it to yourselves.

Reading to Your Child

"What can I do to help my child become a successful reader?" is a frequent question. I begin by explaining that reading is not one skill but the interplay of several:

Inquiry

First and foremost, reading is an act of inquiry, exploration, and discovery. Reading is one of the best ways a child can learn about the workings of the world around him. An inquisitive baby rummages through drawers and cabinets in search of knowledge. In the same way, and for the same reason, an inquisitive toddler rummages through the pages of a book.

Imagination

Reading is an act of imagination. A toddler transforms words into images in the same way he transforms a shoebox into a boat. Imagination is essential to comprehension. It breathes life into the static word, making it dynamic. Without imagination, words are hollow, devoid of meaning. The child who has misplaced her imagination (or had it displaced by television) will approach reading as a chore rather than a joy.

Coordination

Reading involves the coordination of physical and mental processes—hands, eyes, and brain. Hands hold the book, turning the pages and adjusting the depth of field so the eyes can easily scan lines of print, transmitting raw data to the brain. The brain operates actively on that data, decoding, retrieving information stored in its vast data bank, making associations, forming mental images—all of which culminates in the "Ah-ha!" of comprehension.

Competence

Reading, like every other challenge, offers a child the opportunity to grow intellectually, creatively, emotionally, and socially. A successful reader is an inquisitive, imaginative, well-coordinated child.

With all of this in mind, here are two things a parent can do to encourage the growth of reading skills.

- *Provide safe, stimulating environments that encourage the growth of inquiry and imagination.* From his earliest months, if a child's inquiries into the world are rewarding (as opposed to frustrating), if his parents feed (as opposed to deprive) his appetite for discovery, when the time comes he will want to rummage as eagerly through books as he did through drawers and cabinets when he was younger.

- *Spend lots of time reading to your child.* There are few things more completely enriching to a child—emotionally, socially, and intellectually—than being read to. Nestled securely in a parent's arms, listening as he or she paints word-pictures, a child learns that reading feels good. Children follow the examples that parents set. If parents read, a child will follow suit. On the other hand, if parents rely on the television as their primary source of entertainment and information, a child will see little if any value in reading.

Spacing

"How far apart should we space our children?" is another question frequently asked by today's parents. As the size of the average American family has shrunk, concern over the issue of spacing has increased.

Developmental psychologist Burton White has found that three and one-half years is the ideal interval between siblings. Contrary to what many parents think, the chance of problems with the older child and within the sibling relationship increases not only as that ideal interval shortens but also as it lengthens. In other words, parents are just as likely to have problems with a spacing of five years as they are with one and one-half.

The problem with close spacing is that the first child may not yet be ready to do with less parental attention when the second child comes along. When this is the case, the older child's development may stall as he struggles to keep the baby from taking his place in the spotlight. By thirty-six months, most children have achieved a satisfactory degree of autonomy and are not going to be threatened by the arrival of a sibling.

The problem with longer spacing is that the older child has had time to settle comfortably—too comfortably, in fact—into the role of only child. That is his territory, so to speak, within the family, and he isn't willing to share it with anyone else.

For the first eight months of the second-born child's life, his relative passivity and helplessness pose few problems for the first-born. However, as the baby begins to move about independently and make increasing demands on the parents' time and attention, the older child's perception of him begins to change. Where the baby was once cute and cuddly, the older child now begins to see him as an intruder. In the case of close spacing, the older child may become aggressive toward the baby, or he may regress in one or more ways (e.g., baby talk, wetting his pants, wanting to drink from a bottle) in an attempt to reclaim the attention he's lost. When spacing is longer, the older child may exhibit jealousy toward the younger child by ignoring him, refusing to share toys, and teasing.

It's all but inevitable that a toddler will have some difficulty adjusting to a new sibling. Some will have a lot, some just a little. Some start having difficulty several months before the birth of the second child, and others have no problems at all until the baby is crawling. Regardless, problems of one sort or another are almost certain. The good news is they can be minimized with proper planning and management.

Involvement

Include the older child in such things as shopping for baby furniture, decorating the nursery, and talking about names. This will help him feel he's playing an important role in the baby's arrival. The greater his investment along these lines, the more likely it is he will develop feelings of affection toward the baby long before the Big Day. Once baby has arrived, continue to find ways of engaging the older child's help. This will prevent the feeling that he's competing with the baby for your attention.

The underinvolved child may regard the baby as a trespasser, someone he didn't ask for and doesn't especially want. As a result, he will seek ways of discharging his jealousy. These may range from getting into mischief whenever Mom is occupied with feeding or diapering to actual displays of aggression toward the baby. Behaviors such as these are signals from the child that he's feeling left out and needs not just more attention from his parents but more involvement with his new sibling as well.

Plan Ahead

Avoid surprises that might result in feelings of anger or frustration on the part of the older child. For example, don't suddenly give the older child's room to the baby. Make transitions of this sort several months before the baby's arrival.

Talk

Include the firstborn in discussions about the baby. Let him feel the baby's movements. Obtain a stethoscope and let him hear the baby's heartbeat. Show him pictures of himself when he was a newborn. Talk about the responsibilities he'll have toward his new brother or sister. After the baby's arrival, if the first child seems to be having problems, it may help to read him a book that deals with this subject. Knowing he's not alone in the world with these feelings will help him come to grips with them. One of the better books of this genre is *Peter's Chair* by Ezra Jack Keats. In it, Peter talks about how mad he is that his baby sister has moved in and taken his crib and favorite chair. This charming little book shows how Peter resolves this crisis.

Include

Once Mom and baby are home and receiving visitors, encourage friends and relatives to bring a small surprise for the older child, especially if they're coming with a gift for the baby. Also mention to them how important it is that they make a bit of a fuss over the older child as well, congratulating him on how cute his baby brother or sister is and how proud he must be.

By taking these simple steps to support the first child's adjustment to the second, you help set a positive tone in the sibling relationship from the very beginning. That means less jealousy now and less sibling conflict later. That's an offer no parent can refuse!

Questions?

Q *What should we look for when selecting toys for our child, who's now twenty-five months old?*

A The concept of play value is an important one for parents to keep in mind when selecting toys for children. A toy's play value is measured in terms of three characteristics: durability, flexibility, and developmental appropriateness.

Durability: This simply refers to the toy's ability to withstand the wear and tear of a child's play. Since toddlers like to take things apart anyway, it's wise to purchase toys they can take apart without breaking.

Flexibility: A flexible toy can be many things, as opposed to one thing only. Blocks, for example, are flexible, while a wind-up train is not. The more flexible or multidimensional the toy is, the more it will stimulate the child's imagination and promote creative behavior.

Developmental appropriateness: Does the toy match the child's developmental characteristics? Toys that can be disassembled without breaking are developmentally appropriate for toddlers because toddlers like to take things apart. Blocks are a prime example. Toddlers like to build things. Other toys that fit this category are crayons and dolls.

The greater a toy's play value, the longer it will hold a child's interest. It follows that by choosing toys that are high in play value, parents can save money, promote good development, and free up lots of time for themselves.

Q *How can I get my toddler to pick up his toys? When I tell him to pick them up, he just looks at me like I'm speaking gibberish.*

A You're probably asking him to do something that seems overwhelming. If he is a typical American two-year-old, he already has fifty or more toys. He quickly turns this plethora of toys into clutter, at which point you want him to pick them up. Huh? You must be kidding.

Turn a closet or cabinet into a toy lending library. Go through your child's toys, culling ones he no longer plays with. Keep culling until you get down to no more than twenty. Put the rest in the new toy lending closet. From that point on, allow your toddler to play with no more than one or two at a time and make a rule that in order for him to get a toy out of the closet, he must give you one to put back in. This keeps the number of toys that are out at any given time to a number that your child will be able to pick up in no time at all.

Q *What should I look for when choosing books for my two-year-old?*

A More than anything else, you should look for books that interest *you*—books that attract your attention and that you will enjoy reading yourself. The more you enjoy a book, the more enthusiasm you will bring to the act of reading it aloud. The more enthusiasm you bring, the more you will stimulate your child's imagination and language skills, and the more effectively you will communicate to your child the most important message of all: Reading is fun!

In addition, look for books that are durable, colorful, and written in short, simple, yet interesting sentences. In that last regard, keep in mind that toddlers are captivated by rhyme, which is why the Dr. Seuss books are so enduringly popular with children this age (and adults too!).

When reading to your child, bring the story to life by modulating your tone of voice. Consider taking on a different voice for each character, even singing parts of the book. Once your child learns the story, stop at the last word or phrase of certain sentences, letting your child fill it in. Interactive reading of this sort is just another way of hooking your child on books, and the earlier he's hooked, the better.

Q *Our first child is eighteen months old. When should we begin reading to her?*

A About a year ago. Seriously, a child is never too young to be read to. Parents should begin reading to a child by six months of age, but if you had started reading to your daughter when she was a few days old, it would have been even better.

When I was reading to my children, I generally preferred books with lots and lots of pictures because that forced us to cuddle. The pictures also became the occasion for games of "Show me" and "What's this?"

Early reading stimulates language development, imagination, and cognitive growth. In addition, studies have shown that as a child's communication skills improve, so does motor coordination. This makes sense, not only because an enriching environment stimulates a child's abilities in all areas but also because language development and motor behavior are interwoven during early childhood. The nurturing that takes place when a parent reads to a child also helps strengthen the child's sense of security, which in turn contributes greatly to the development of independence. The bottom line: Early (and ongoing) reading is one of the best investments you can make in your child's well-being.

But don't confuse reading to your daughter with teaching her to read. When you sit down to read to her, do so because it's something you both enjoy. If you start reading to her now, and read to her often, she will learn that reading is enjoyable, and that's sufficient.

Q *We are the parents of a perfectly happy, outgoing boy of fifteen months. We regularly dress in front of him and take baths with him. Up until now, he hasn't acted overly interested in our private parts, but we'd like some guidance for the future. Is there a point at which we should stop appearing nude in front of him? How should we answer him when he asks questions about our bodies? When he's four or five, but still needs help with his bath, will he be embarrassed to have us bathe him?*

A Here are the bare facts: At this age, there's nothing inappropriate in what you're doing with and in front of your son. At some point in the near future, he will surely become interested in your private parts. When he asks, "What's this?" answer him as casually as if he pointed to your chin.

Concerning what to call these body parts, there are those who insist that parents should answer with none other than proper anatomical terms. Excepting vulgarities, there's really nothing to fret over either way. Words like "winky" and "bumbum" are perfectly okay and no more misleading than calling the child's stomach a "tummy."

Sometime between his third and fourth birthdays, your son will begin developing what's known as gender identity. He will realize that girls and boys are physically different and that not only is he a boy, but he is like his daddy in this respect. This is the appropriate time to introduce the concept of modesty. From that point on, you should be more circumspect about appearing nude in front of him. I'm not suggesting that you become neurotic about nudity, just prudent. After all, it's impossible for several people to live together in close quarters without seeing at least occasional glimpses of one another's unclothed bodies. The older your son gets, the more you should expect him to respect your privacy, and the more you should respect his.

Four is a good age at which to discontinue the practice of taking baths with him. You can use the excuse that he's too big for the both of you to fit comfortably in the tub at the same time.

Q *We are very health-conscious parents who want our eighteen-month-old daughter to grow up physically fit. There's an exercise program for toddlers at a local health club, and we'd like to know your feelings about such things.*

A Aren't toddlers active enough as it is? I know mine were. By the time they were eighteen months old, they were climbing bookcases, escaping from their cribs, jumping on furniture, throwing food, and running away from us in stores, airports, and other crowded places. They got plenty of exercise, and so did we. Who needs more active babies? None of the parents I know.

Not only are baby exercise programs unnecessary, they're downright dangerous to the mental health of parents! I can see it now: As the baby exercise craze sweeps the nation, we begin hearing reports of nine-month-olds vaulting out of their play-pens, twelve-month-olds escaping down crib-sheet ropes from their bedroom windows, and eighteen-month-olds running merrily through the streets with their parents in hot, panting pursuit, going slowly but aerobically insane.

Yes, infants and toddlers should get plenty of exercise, and they will, pretty much on their own, as long as parents and other caregivers provide environments that are safe, stimulating, and allow for plenty of movement, exploration, and manipulation. Baby exercise classes are no substitute for a home that recognizes the growing child's need for activity and, within reasonable boundaries, allows for it.

Q *The latest rage among the mommies in my community is yoga for toddlers. The advertising promises all sort of benefits. What are your thoughts?*

A Intrigued by this question, I did some investigating and discovered that many of these programs are based on the writing of Helen Garabedian, the author of *Itsy Bitsy Yoga for Toddlers and Preschoolers* (De Capo Press, 2008). *Newsweek* once called Garabedian the "Baby Yoga Expert." The hype for her book promises fewer tantrums, better sleep, better motor coordination, improved listening ability, improved ability to follow directions, better self-expression, and higher self-esteem. Oh, puh-leeze!

Many of these same benefits, and more, are going to result from taking a child to the park for a couple of hours several times a week and letting him run and play on the equipment. Besides, the park is free. As for fewer tantrums and enhanced obedience, sorry, but yoga is no substitute for calm, firm discipline.

Garabedian's publicity also claims that according to research, toddlers need thirty minutes of "structured activity" per day. I pride myself on staying on top of stuff like this, and I know of no such research. In fact, the only research I'm aware of says that toddlers benefit more from unstructured than structured play. The one thing today's youngsters do not need is more micro-management, more structure, and less discretionary time. I give toddler yoga an emphatic two thumbs down.

Q *Our daughter, who just turned two, has started asking me "Why?" about almost everything. She'll ask me a question like, "What's this?" (pointing to a picture in a book). I'll answer and she'll ask "Why?" I don't want her to stop asking questions, but sometimes I feel like a nonstop answer machine. How should I be handling this?*

A You must first realize that simply because your daughter can ask "Why?" doesn't mean she can understand the answer. For instance, let's say she points to a picture of the sun going down and asks, "What's this?" You say, "It's a picture of the sun going down," to which she asks, "Why?" I guarantee that no amount of explaining will cause her to understand why the sun seems to disappear over the edge of the earth every evening. At age two, she's probably able to comprehend the answers to very few of her "Why?" questions. But as you've discovered, comprehend or not, she's going to keep on asking.

The never-ending "Why?" is typical of an intelligent two-year-old. It is a request for information. Therefore, you should give information, but it isn't necessary that the response be scientifically correct. In fact, your answer can be total fiction as long as it relates in some way to the original question. For example, if your daughter asks why the sun goes down, you can answer, "Because it's tired and needs to sleep," or "Because it's playing peekaboo with you." One answer is really as good as the next. It's even all right to give a different answer every time your daughter asks the same question.

Your daughter keeps asking "Why?" because she is beginning to understand cause and effect. This is an exciting discovery, and she wants to know as much about it as she can. But it's enough that you simply confirm for her that, "Yes, there's a reason for that, too!" In addition, it's important that the answer be in terms she *can* understand. In most cases, that eliminates the "correct" answer as a possibility.

If you think that what I'm suggesting is tantamount to lying to her, take a look at the books you read to her. In them, there are fantastic creatures and trees that talk and all manner of impossible things. The point is that it's not necessary for you to describe the world to young children in correct terms, only that you describe it in terms they can relate to and comprehend. If it were vital that young children always hear correct answers and descriptions, we'd read to them from the encyclopedia instead of a storybook.

Realize, also, that the repetitive "Why?" is the beginning of conversation. It's verbal give-and-take at its most basic level. And again, the give-and-take, the process, is far more important than the content of your answers. When you've had enough, change the subject by asking *her* a question or giving her something to do.

Q *Our first child, an eighteen-month-old daughter, has recently started clinging to me (her mother), following me from room to room, and wanting to be held more than ever. I thought children became more independent as they got older. Have I done something to make her insecure?*

A Children *do* become more independent as they get older, but sometimes independence grows in a two-steps-forward, one-step-backward fashion. This is one of those times.

Envision yourself venturing out to explore a dark, deserted house, one that has both attracted and repelled you with its mystery. You open the door and stand there for a while until your eyes adjust to the dim light. Then you take a few steps into the house and stop. Hearing a creak, you retreat back to the front door until you are reassured that all is safe. Taking a few more steps into the house than before, you once again stop and listen. Then you take a few more steps, and again you stop. Every time you hear something that sets your heart pounding, you retreat to the last safe place you occupied until the coast is clear.

And so it goes with your daughter, who has begun the process of self-discovery. Up until now, she has not had a sense of her own identity. As self-consciousness begins to develop and the drive toward independence awakens, she is thrown into conflict. To become a person in her own right, she must leave the safety of her relationship with you and venture into uncharted yet compelling territory. Intuitively she knows that once she takes those steps, nothing will ever again be the same between you. Before she puts this distance between herself and you, she must first be absolutely certain that you will still be there whenever she feels the need for reassurance.

No, you haven't made your daughter insecure. In order to achieve a state of independence, she must learn to accept and deal with insecurity. Research has shown that the more available and reassuring mothers are during this stage, the better. Even though your daughter's clinging and following may be oppressive at times, it's best to allow it. A child who has trouble getting back "Home" again won't want to leave. Let her cling, and she will eventually cling less. Let her follow, and she will follow less. Hold her when she wants, and she will eventually ask to be held less. Believe me, there'll come a day when you'll wish she asked you to hold her more often.

Q *My thirty-three-month-old daughter has suddenly developed a fear of going outside. If I try to take her outside to play, go for a walk, or even go down the street to see a friend, she begins to scream. She isn't able to tell me what she's afraid of, nor do I have a clue. I'm home with her during the day and nothing traumatic has happened that might explain this. Do you have some idea as to what might be going on here?*

A The sudden onset of strange and inexplicable fears is not at all unusual in older toddlers and threes. The parent of an almost-three-year-old once told me her son had become deathly afraid of newspapers and would flee hysterically from any room in which he discovered one. Other parents have recounted equally peculiar stories of older toddlers developing fears of birds, bushes, flashlights, and running water. And of course, there are the usual fears of the dark, thunder, and dogs.

All of this is normal, I assure you. The child's imagination—the first stirring of abstract thought—is beginning to flower at this age. Previously, things were exactly as they seemed. Outside was outside; newspapers were newspapers. Now, however, as imagination begins to play games with pure sensory experience, perception becomes a matter of interpretation. Outside becomes a threatening place, and newspapers—perhaps because of the crinkling, popping noises of their pages being turned—become living things capable of who knows what. We can romanticize this leap of consciousness as mind-expanding, but it introduces a dimension to the child's perception of reality that can be frightening.

Your daughter needs to feel a sense of absolute confidence in your ability to control a world that's suddenly become threatening. You must act as if you know exactly what you're doing.

Accept her fears but do not participate in them. Don't ask her why she's afraid. She won't be able to tell you, and whatever words you put in her mouth will only worsen her anxieties. And don't discredit her fears by saying "That's silly," or similar statements.

If she suddenly tells you she's afraid of monsters, don't tell her there's no such thing. At this age, a child cannot understand why a word exists for something that does not. If she wants to talk about what's frightening her, just listen. When it's your turn to talk, say, "Everything's all right. Mommy and Daddy are here to take care of you, and we will!"

The only way she's going to stop being afraid is if you help her confront the very thing she fears most. If you don't have to leave the house for any other purpose during the day, take her on a walk around the neighborhood. Don't ask if she wants to go, just take her. If she screams, just hold her and remind her that everything's all right, that you are taking care of her. Given an adequate display of control on your part, this crisis will run its course in short order.

Q *Our thirty-four-month-old son has suddenly become afraid of the dark. He won't stay in his bedroom at night because he thinks there's a monster under his bed. Our solution has been to let him fall asleep on the sofa and move him to his bed when he's asleep. A psychiatrist acquaintance of ours said this was an "obvious manipulation" on our son's part, an "attempt to control us." What do you think?*

A I think the statement made by the psychiatrist is an obvious manipulation on his part, an attempt to control *you*. Fears are common at this age. Leading the list is a fear of the dark, including the belief that malevolent creatures lurk therein. At this age, fears result from the interaction of three related factors:

- *The need to protect a fragile sense of identity.* As a child grows in self-sufficiency, he must learn to handle the anxiety that comes with letting go of his parents. Fears dramatize this process. They are symbolic, fantasy-driven expressions of the young child's emotional vulnerability.
- *The flowering of imaginative thought.* This age child is able to conjure up mental images of things real and unreal, but he isn't able to discriminate between the two. Whatever he can see in his mind is no less real to him than the things he sees in his front yard.
- *The inseparability of word and thing.* In the mind of an older toddler, if something has a name, then it must exist. The idea that there are words for things that don't exist is incomprehensible at this age. This is why any attempt to talk a toddler or three-year-old out of fears won't work. The rational explanation and the fear are on separate wavelengths.

Problems concerning a young child's fears arise because parents often misinterpret them as expressions of insecurity or upcoming emotional problems. The parents then begin responding to the child's fears with guilt and anxiety. Their attempts to compensate for the "damage" simply increase the child's confusion and sense of helplessness. The more anxious the parents become, the more fearful the child becomes. Their reactions reinforce the fear and confirm it as something real. If there is nothing to be afraid of, thinks the child, then why are Mommy and Daddy acting so afraid?

The most effective approach involves a few steps. First, acknowledge the fear ("I know the dark can be scary when you're little"). Second, identify with your son ("When I was little, I was afraid, too"). Third, reassure him of your ability to protect him. You can also help him overcome his fright by playing on the talent that created it—namely, his imagination. Have him relax and look at a blank wall. Then, tell him to think about a tall, handsome prince on a beautiful white horse (be very descriptive). Say, "This prince, named Bojangles, is your friend. If you call his name, he will come into your room and chase the monster away. While you sleep, he will stand guard over your bed and keep the monster away." Use *your* imagination to elaborate on this or any similar idea and plant it firmly in your son's mind.

Far-fetched? Not to a young child. If he can conjure up a monster, he can conjure up a guardian prince. And have lots of fun to boot!

Q *Our thirty-two-month-old daughter has recently invented an imaginary playmate whom she calls Cindy. Her obsession with this new friend is going a bit far, I think. She sometimes wants me to set a place at the table for Cindy and never fails to bring her along any time we leave the house. When I've suggested that Cindy isn't real, my daughter has become angry and upset, so I've dropped it. Do I have reason to be concerned, or is this just a passing phase?*

A Your daughter's fascination with Cindy is just a passing phase, but it's a very important one. Rather than being worried, you should be glad. Fantasy thinking emerges in the late twos or early threes. Like any other mental attribute, imagination must be exercised in order to strengthen and grow. Cindy provides your daughter with the opportunity to do just that. This is a very important step toward the eventual mastery of abstract thinking ability. Also, since imagination is essential to reading comprehension, Cindy is actually helping your daughter become a successful reader.

Trying to debate the issue of Cindy's existence with your daughter is a lost cause. In her eyes and mind, Cindy is as real as you are. Furthermore, young children invest a considerable amount of security in their imaginary playmates. They need them. No wonder your daughter became upset when you denied Cindy's existence. Just as your adult mind cannot comprehend your daughter's obsession with Cindy, your daughter cannot comprehend your failure to accept her. So call it a draw and stop worrying.

Cindy is also helping your daughter develop social skills. This is timely, because at this age, your daughter is beginning to form relationships with other children. Cindy enables her to practice social skills in a safe, nonthreatening context.

The more your daughter plays with Cindy, the fewer demands she makes of you. Instead of looking to you for occupation, she is relying on Cindy, which effectively means she is depending on herself. The more self-reliant and resourceful your daughter becomes, the better sense of self-esteem she will have.

Any way you look at it, Cindy is one of the best things that's ever happened to your daughter. Her invisible friend is contributing to almost every aspect of her growth and development. Instead of worrying about her "obsession," relax and count your blessings.

Q *We have a son who is nearly three and an eight-month-old daughter. All of a sudden, our son wants to drink from a bottle, wear diapers during the day, and be rocked to sleep. Despite several tantrums, we haven't given in to these demands. Now he's started wetting his pants during the day, something he hasn't done in six months. What should we do about this?*

A Your job is to reassure your son that his place in the family may be different and changing, but it's still secure and protected. You must also convince him, firmly but gently, that the time for bottles, being rocked to sleep, and wearing diapers has passed. The next time he wets his pants, have him help you clean up the spill.

Then, take him to the bathroom and teach him to rinse out his wet clothing and drape it over the tub to dry. This isn't punishment, and you shouldn't communicate it as such. Furthermore, you needn't be overly concerned with how good a job he does. You are only making him responsible for his accident and showing him you won't give in on the diaper issue.

Q *We have two children, ages five and two, with a third on the way. Which of the two children is more likely to have problems with the new arrival, and what, if anything, can we do to prevent them?*

A Your two-year-old will have to make more of an adjustment to the new sibling than the five-year-old. The reason for this is simple: When the third child arrives, the five-year-old will retain his status as the oldest, but for the two-year-old, everything will change. He will have to relinquish his role as the "baby" to his new brother or sister and become instead the middle child. This shuffling of roles causes what amounts to an identity crisis and often results in the attention-seeking behavior characteristic of "middle child syndrome." A study in conflict and contradiction, the middle child ends up wanting the best of both his older and younger siblings' worlds. He wants the freedom and privilege given the oldest, as well as the attention given the youngest. To keep this conflict at a minimum, involve the two-year-old as much as possible in preparing for the third child's arrival. Once he or she is here, find ways your two-year-old can help you take care of the baby. The more important you make him feel in his own right, the less he'll strive for attention in inappropriate ways.

Q *Our thirty-month-old has recently started hitting, pushing, and squeezing his ten-month-old sister. What's causing this, and how should we handle it?*

A Your son's aggression results from a combination of jealousy, territorial instincts, and clumsy attempts to play with his sister. Your first order of business is to protect the baby. Your second is to guide your son into a more gentle relationship with her. Begin by putting her completely off-limits to your son. For at least a week, don't allow him to hold, touch, or even come near her. During this time, have him help you by getting things and doing things for you while you're involved with the baby. After a week or so, begin allowing your son brief moments of closely supervised contact with his sister—getting toys for her, helping you change her, and so on. Praise him for being gentle and helpful. As time goes on, increase the frequency and kind of contact you allow him to have with her. If your son hurts the baby, sit him in a time-out chair for a few minutes. If he says he's sorry, simply say, "I know you are, but you must learn to be gentle with your baby sister." This will almost certainly be a two-steps-forward, one-step-back process for at least several weeks. Eventually, however, your patience and consistency will pay off. (See chapter 6 for more on this subject.)

Q *My husband and I separated several months ago. Ever since, our usually outgoing, happy thirty-four-month-old daughter has been clinging and whiny. She wants to be with me all the time. If I tell her to stop following me around, she begins to cry. Almost every day, she asks when her daddy is coming back. He's not, but I'm worried that the truth will upset her even more. What should I be doing to help her through this crisis?*

A Just after a separation, young children will often cling almost desperately to the remaining parent. Preschoolers—boys as well as girls—tend to be more dependent on their mothers than their fathers. Nevertheless, your husband's presence in the home was essential to your daughter's picture of the family as a constant, unchanging unit. Her father's departure altered this picture and disrupted her sense of security. In response, she clings to you as if to say, "Don't you leave me, too!"

This is no doubt an extremely vulnerable time for you as well. Your security has been turned upside down, and your emotional resources are stretched to their limit. Under the circumstances, it may be difficult for you to respond patiently to your daughter's overpowering need for reassurance. A vicious cycle may be developing: The more anxious you are, the more anxious your daughter becomes; the more insecure she acts, the more anxious you become; and so on. If you feel caught up in this cycle, it may be wise for you to see an experienced family counselor. A competent professional can help you stabilize your new family situation.

Under the circumstances, it isn't unusual for a child to regress to behaviors typical of earlier stages of growth—behaviors associated with safety and security. Your daughter's clinging is one example of this. If she wants to be held, and you can hold her, hold her. If you cannot hold her at that moment, tell her why and try to redirect her attention to something else until your hands are free. In other words, be as responsive as you can possibly be to her, but don't let her take control of the relationship.

Answer her questions clearly and honestly. Don't editorialize about the separation. Just stick to the facts. Tell her that Daddy is going to live somewhere else, but don't try to explain why. Tell her what role her daddy will continue to play in her life, and remember that he will continue to play an important role in your life as well. In the long run, the best thing for your daughter is to have two parents who do their best to put aside their animosities and make every effort to communicate often and well.

Q *I'm having trouble getting my twenty-month-old son to give up drinking from a bottle. He drinks from a cup at meals and during the day, but cries for his bottle whenever he's upset or sleepy. Should I refuse to give it to him?*

A There is much to lose and nothing to be gained by struggling with your son over whether he can have his bottle when he feels the need for it. When we make issues out of things like bottles and thumbs and security blankets, children are likely to become more desperate in their attachment to them. Allow your son to drink from a bottle whenever he expresses the need for that source of comfort. Handled nonchalantly, this will pass in short order.

Security blankets, thumbs, pacifiers, and the like are known as *transitional objects*. They help young children feel secure enough to make the leap from one level of development to the next. Despite the prejudiced view parents tend to have of them, these things are actually a parent's best friend. A child who carries a security blanket with him to preschool is more likely to separate easily from his parents. A child who's allowed to suck his thumb will self-comfort when frustrated.

At times, it may make practical sense to limit a child's access to transitional objects, but children will give them up more quickly if parents don't prohibit them altogether. For example, parents might tell a child he can carry his security blanket to preschool, but he must give it to the teacher once he arrives. Likewise, parents might tell a child he can have his pacifier only at naptime and bedtime. In any case, a child is not going to lose interest in a transitional object as long as his or her parents act as if it's the biggest deal in the world.

Q *Our daughter is nearly three. She's sucked her thumb since the day she was born. The dentist assures us that she isn't sucking hard enough to cause a serious orthodontic problem, so we aren't in a panic over it. Basically, we allow her to suck whenever she wants to, which is mostly when she's bored or upset. Lately, however, we've become concerned that perhaps our permissiveness might backfire on her when she gets to school and encounters ridicule and criticism from other children and* *maybe even teachers. Should we begin to try to stop her thumb sucking now, and if so, how?*

A   If your daughter's thumb sucking isn't resulting in dental problems, and if it hasn't been a battle up until now, why make it one? And a battle is what you'll surely have if you try to make her stop.

My theory is that the more parents try to stop a child from thumb sucking, the more determined the child becomes, and the more pressure the child will apply to the palate, thereby increasing the chances of future orthodontic problems. So don't try to stop your daughter from sucking her thumb. She enjoys it, it's harmless, and she uses her thumb to comfort herself when she's upset. When she begins school, she'll become quickly aware of and responsive to what her peers think of her habit.

Q   *My husband and I have a two-year-old son who is in a very clingy phase. Three months ago he had a very bad episode of separation anxiety when we changed his sleeping situation. Since then, he's been very Mommy-oriented. He wants me to do everything for him and screams and fights if Daddy tries to do even the smallest thing. During the day, however, he's perfectly fine with his regular sitter. In two weeks, I have to go away on business for a few days. Is there anything I can do between now and then to make my being away easier for him or prepare him for it? I've read about a lot of gimmicky things but didn't know if any of it would work.*

A   My nongimmicky advice, strange and counterintuitive as it may sound, is for you to simply disappear. Long goodbyes, an attempt on your part to explain where you're going and how long you're going to be gone, will do nothing but create drama and set the stage for a very difficult separation for both you and your son. He will understand only that you are anxious, and you are leaving, and he's not going along. The inevitable consequence will be lots of angst.

A number of years ago, our daughter-in-law brought two-year-old Thomas to visit us for a couple of days while she went to a wedding. Grandma Willie told me that Thomas was very "clingy" and "attached to Mom" and would certainly have difficulty separating from Nancy at the point of exchange—the airport. Knowing Nancy, I doubted that, but having learned many invaluable lessons in my many years of marriage, I said nothing.

I met Nancy and Thomas as they got off the plane. As we walked to the car, where Grandma was waiting, I told Nancy this needed to be quick. She agreed. At the car, she buckled Thomas into his car seat, kissed him, and closed the door. We drove away. It took Thomas about five minutes to realize Mommy wasn't in the car, at which point his face started scrunching up and he got the sniffles. Grandma and I just started talking to him about all the wonderful things we were going to do, and he stopped. Two days later, Nancy arrived to retrieve a perfectly content two-year-old.

By the way, you and your husband have absolutely got to stop letting a toddler decide which parent does things for him. How does a twenty-something-pound two-year-old not allow his father to do things for him? He screams? He struggles? He acts like he's having the toddler equivalent of a panic attack? Pay no attention. Dad should simply go right ahead and do what he came to do. He should ignore the screaming, the panic, and so on, and you should do the same.

"Yes, Daddy's going to change you. Oh, that's all right. There, there. Everything's all right, but you can scream if you want to. That's just fine. Daddy loves you, yes I do."

You and your husband will eventually pay a heavy price if you do not get control of the relationship now.

Q *Our two-year-old isn't talking yet, and we're worried to death about it. He babbles, and it's obvious that he's trying to say words, but he doesn't say anything intelligible except "ma-ma" and "da-da." Every other developmental marker is on schedule. We've had his hearing tested, and his pediatrician says everything's okay and not to worry. What should we do?*

A You should listen to the pediatrician. Stop worrying. If your son's hearing is fine, and he's attempting speech, then he'll talk in his own time. Indeed, your son's a bit behind the curve—a bit, mind you—in his speech development, but that's not unusual for boys. The norm is established by counting in all the girls, and the average girl begins talking intelligibly three to six months earlier than the average boy. According to rumor, Albert Einstein didn't talk until he was three. My first grandson, who graduated high school near the top of his class, didn't begin talking intelligibly until he was almost three.

 If your son were not even attempting speech, I'd be giving you a more cautious answer, but everything sounds fine to me. As you point out, everything but language development is proceeding on schedule. Although a significant speech delay in combination with other developmental delays may indicate a serious problem, a slight delay in language development alone isn't worth worrying about.

Q *My two-and-one-half-year-old sometimes becomes obsessed with certain objects or activities. When this happens, it's impossible to distract him or redirect him. If I try to get him to focus on something else, he gets really agitated. If I put him in time-out, he'll calm down, but he usually starts right back up again when his time is up. Is this sort of obsessive behavior normal at this age, or is it something that needs to be addressed?*

A If by "addressed" you are asking whether he might need some sort of professional evaluation or therapy, the answer is no. The behavior in question is not unusual for toddlers. Quite simply, your son becomes upset because he can't understand why you're so determined to pull him away from something that fascinates him. The fact is, the more you attempt to stop his obsessing either by redirecting or punishing, the more determined he's likely to become.

As it is, you're turning this into a power struggle of sorts, but his behavior justifies nothing more than good-humored ignoring. If he wants you to participate in the obsessing, do so. Show great interest in what he's trying to show you or do. This will run its course quickly if you just relax and roll with it.

Q *In my hometown, various enrichment programs for children under three are proliferating. A two-year-old can take ballet, music, yoga, or join a soccer team, among other options. I've always considered these classes a waste of money, but I worry that I might be setting my toddler up for a lifetime of mediocrity (which is the implication in the literature of many of these programs) if I don't put her in one or more of these classes right now. Is there any real benefit to these programs, or are they a general waste of money?*

A My short answer is that children developed the skills in question before any of these programs existed. These courses capitalize on anxiety that mothers have about their children "keeping up" with their peers, but no good, objective evidence exists to suggest that children who are not enrolled in them fall behind their peers developmentally. The child who is destined to be a great musician, given opportunity and sufficient support, will become a great musician. That likelihood is not increased if the child is enrolled in a music program as a toddler. Save your money and use your time and your child's more wisely.

Q *I have recently assigned an evening dishwashing chore to our just-turned-three-year-old. He's quite capable of doing the job; the only problem is that he gets easily sidetracked. He quickly becomes caught up in some elaborate fantasy involving soap, water, and the dishes. So it takes him a long time to get the three plates, cups, and silverware washed. I don't feel quite right punishing him, but I do tell him that he used up all his after-dinner playtime doing his chore, and now it is time for bed. Will he get the hang of this in time, or should I do something different?*

A First, congratulations. You are one of a dwindling minority of parents who actually believe that young children are truly capable. You have proven that not only can older toddlers be trusted to do basic household chores, but also that there is hope still left in the world.

As for his imagination getting in the way of his focus, it's not a problem at all. A child's imagination is in full flower at this time in his life. Three-year-olds can easily become lost in their imaginings no matter what they're doing. Since imagination is the root of all creativity, not to mention fun, I encourage you to be content with the fact that he eventually finishes his chore. The fact that he's used up most of his evening by the time he finishes is of no consequence to him. After all, he's just had more fun than adults can imagine. Sometimes, one encourages growth in a child by simply staying out of it.

Q *I've heard that reading to a young child, even during the first year of life, teaches the value of reading and even stimulates brain development. But every time I attempt to read to my eighteen-month-old son he grabs the book away, closes it, or wants to flip the pages himself. If I try to take it back, the battle is on, one that I do not wish to engage in.*

A Yes, reading to a child from an early age is beneficial in many ways. It stimulates a child's interest in books, enriches imagination, enhances language development, provides a setting for a very nurturing parent–child experience, and stimulates the growing brain. But I'd simply wait until your son is older and try again.

My entire recommendation is as follows: Parents should read to a child from an early age as long as the child is willing to sit still and pay attention and obviously wants to be read to (goes and gets books and asks a parent to read to him), and the experience is enjoyable for both parent and child. If all those conditions are not yet in place by eighteen months, there is absolutely nothing to worry about. Just keep offering the opportunity to your son. Don't push. And stop worrying. Believe me, if he's not receptive to the experience for another year, that will not make any difference in the long run.

Q *My husband and I are raising our two-year-old grandson. He's been in day care since he was a year old. He loves his current day care, and we've had absolutely no problems until recently. All of a sudden, when I drop him off, he has started clinging and crying and asking me not to go to work. I can't figure out why this is happening, because as soon as I leave (after hugging him and reassuring him that I'm coming back), he's fine, and during the day he plays well with the other kids. I stayed at home with my children, so I've never experienced this problem with a child. Should I be looking for some underlying issue, or is this perfectly normal?*

A Separation anxiety can arise spontaneously at this age, with no cause whatsoever. If handled calmly and matter-of-factly by the child's parents, it should pass within a few months at most. In the meantime, the longer you stick around at the day care center trying to calm him, the worse any given episode is likely to be.

On the way to the center, tell him what you're doing that day and that you're coming back for him. When you get there, just hand him over, kiss him, tell him you'll see him later, and walk away. Let the teacher deal with any crying that occurs. The sooner you leave, the better. Obviously, his distress passes quickly, as soon as he gets in with the other kids. If he screamed all day or curled up in a fetal position and stayed that way after you left, there'd be reason for concern. So don't worry, be happy!

Q *My nearly three-year-old son has been at home with me since day one. I'm worried about his social development. He loves being around other children his age, but that doesn't often happen. None of my friends have kids his age, and we can't afford preschool. During the day, he spends his time playing with toy trucks and cars and riding his tricycle around the house. He plays very well on his own without any help, but I try to get him outside for a walk or to the park every day, and of course, I read to him a fair amount. He doesn't complain of being bored, but I worry that he might be. Do I need to spend more time playing with him to make up for the lack of kids his age?*

A Your little guy hardly sounds bored to me. He entertains himself well, stays out from underfoot, and sits still when you read to him. Overall, it sounds like he's adjusted to his circumstances quite well. Furthermore, I don't think his social skills are at risk. This is a much overblown issue these days. Preschool is not necessary for healthy personality or social development. In fact, researchers have discovered a connection between aggression and group care during the early years. If your son plays well with other kids, however rarely, he's fine. My prescription: Stop worrying.

Q *My daughter turns three soon, and she is going to have a minor surgical procedure next month. Because she is so young, they are admitting her to the hospital overnight. How should I prepare her for this?*

A The more of a buildup you give the hospital stay, the more anxiety you will generate. Your daughter will not understand any attempt on your part to explain what's going to happen, and it will scare her that she doesn't understand. Also, she will sense your anxiety, and you will have a problem where none would have existed.

The morning of the procedure, say, "We're going to the doctor's today. He's in a new office, in the hospital." Tell her that by helping the doctor, she will get the "ice cream for a week" award for being such a good little girl for the doctor! After the procedure is over and done with, you can and should explain to her what happened.

Q *As a result of being born with a physical defect, my two-year-old daughter has had numerous facial and eye operations. Because of all the stress, she is very attached to me. Her brothers are eighteen, thirteen, and nine. Some days she will choose one of them to be close to, her usual favorite being the oldest. She seems to have a particular dislike for the thirteen-year-old. He tries desperately to give her a hug or read to or play with her, but she'll have nothing to do with him. She also has a similar dislike for her father. On the other hand, she is very secure in going to any nursery or Sunday school program run by women and likes to play with little girls. I think all this is related to the early stress brought on by her medical condition, but how do we get her to show love toward her brother and her father?*

A The fact that your daughter is selective about which members of the family she chooses to reject says that this issue is not directly related to the medical problems of her infancy. Besides, I've heard of selective rejection syndrome developing in young children who've had no early health problems.

The more likely explanation has to do with the huge amount of attention she received and is obviously still receiving from family members. Under the circumstances, even a young child learns how to sustain a cyclone of concern swirling around her. I'm not suggesting that your daughter is manipulating the family. She's much too young to be thinking this through. I suspect this issue came about by accident and was simply one of many that could have developed otherwise.

It's possible that one day she may have become upset when her father or brother tried to pick her up and cuddle with her. Everyone present reacted with great concern, and the dominoes began falling. From there, the more selective she became about affection, the more concern and attention she received, and the more selective she became.

The solution—a variation on reverse psychology—is for your husband and her brother to stop making any affectionate overtures toward her. If they virtually ignore her, your daughter will begin to want attention from them. From now on, I recommend that everyone begin treating her as if she's simply another child instead of a special case who needs to be handled with kid gloves.

Q *How important is it that I provide my two-year-old with socialization opportunities? The other mothers in the neighborhood have formed a play group for their toddlers, but they seem to spend most of their time intervening in squabbles and conflicts over toys.*

A The anxiety endemic to modern mother culture makes it difficult for moms to just go with the flow of their children's development. I am unable to find research that supports the need for contrived social opportunities during toddlerhood. In fact, the research suggests that toddler play groups may contribute to later aggressiveness. As you point out, toddlers are territorial, and in groups they tend to have more conflict than not. This stage works itself out quite naturally sometime during the fourth year of life. Therefore, play groups for three-year-olds make a lot more sense than play groups for twos, but having anxious moms hovering about is counterproductive. It would be much better if your two-year-old had a couple of three-hour weekly sessions at a nonacademic play school.

The mother of a toddler once shared this pertinent testimonial: "My gut was telling me that these organized play group outings were just not necessary and way more trouble than they were worth. When I finally opted out of play date society, life immediately became more enjoyable. I now feel that a little social time at Mothers' Morning Out or church nursery is more than sufficient at this age. I just don't have the time or energy to watch toddlers go at each other over a toy. Both of my kids began sharing spontaneously shortly after their third birthdays, at which time I began accepting play dates again."

Let those with ears hear!

CHAPTER

Creative Discipline

"My eighteen-month-old gets into everything and manages to stay two steps ahead of me, no matter what I do!" said her mother, looking bedraggled, as parents of toddlers often do. "She hits the deck running in the morning and, her nap aside, keeps me going until her bedtime, which comes none too soon."

"I suppose our two-and-a-half-year-old son is what you'd call a strong-willed child," his father told me, as if finally willing to speak the unspeakable. "Anytime things don't go his way, he flops on the floor and begins to scream and thrash about. If we try to comfort him, he scratches, hits, pulls our hair, tries to bite us. It's this Jekyll-and-Hyde thing. One minute he's this lovable, playful kid; the next, he's the Son of Satan."

"Last month, my two-year-old suddenly decided he was no longer going to do anything I asked," his mother complained, dark circles under her eyes. "If I tell him *not* to do something, he does it, all the while looking at me with this gleam in his eye. If I tell him to *stop* doing something, he keeps right on doing it. If I tell him to *do* something, he looks at me like I've got my nerve and says, 'No!' That's all, just 'No!'"

These parents' woeful tales are the stuff of life with two-year-olds. They get into everything, scream when they don't get their way, do what you tell 'em not to do and refuse to do what you tell 'em *to* do. Not all two-year-olds are like this, mind you. Some are sweet and lovable and never present a single problem. My theory is that these rare children are really aliens from another planet who are hiding in the bodies of human children, trying their best not to draw attention to themselves.

All this running amok and screaming and stubbornness is intimidating to parents. For some, it's downright scary. Some parents react to this intimidation, this scariness, by caving in. They get into a routine of trying to figure out what will make their little ones happy. They think that good parents have happy children, so they do whatever it takes to keep their children on an even keel. In no time flat, these children are in complete control of their families.

Other parents react to this intimidation by trying to out-intimidate their children. They scream, threaten to spank, spank, scream, threaten to spank, spank, and so on. When their children are in their early teens, these parents are still screaming and threatening. They never get anywhere because they never learn. Their children? Who knows? The lucky ones, perhaps because of understanding grandparents or teachers, make it. After all, human children are incredibly resilient.

In both cases, these parents take their children's screaming and stubbornness personally. The first group appeases and caters because they think they've done something wrong to make their children act this way. The second group takes their children's behavior as a personal affront, a symptom of ingratitude or something. They become determined to punish this ingratitude into oblivion.

Before we go any further, let's get something straight: Behavior of the above sort, no matter how extreme, is normal for this age. It doesn't mean there's anything wrong with the child, nor does it mean there's anything wrong with the parents of the child. Remember, we're talking about children who think they're the center of the universe. From their point of view, no one has a right to tell them what to do, or deny them what they want, or even delay giving it to them.

If you thought you were the center of the universe, and the people in your life had been cooperating in that delusion for however long and then decided to stop cooperating and begin describing the world to you in realistic terms, you'd scream, too. And you would refuse to acknowledge they were right. You'd be demanding and defiant and generally difficult to live with.

So our subject, before he can accept that he is *not* the center of the universe, must make one last-ditch, pull-out-all-the-stops effort to assert that he is! Such is life, folks. Things always get worse before they get better. At this point, as I mentioned in the *Introduction,* the job of the child's parents is that of demonstrating to him, firmly but gently, that he's just like everyone else, a little fish in a big pond.

If you understand why two-year-olds act the way they do, there's no reason to become either intimidated or angry. Understanding enables acceptance. If you understand and accept stereotypical toddler behavior, it becomes funny—well, sometimes, sort of. If you accept it, then this, too, will pass. If you can't accept it, this behavior is likely to become a perpetual issue. Unfettered of anxiety and anger, you can see the big picture, communicate clearly, position yourself properly, keep your balance, and do the job God wants you to do and humankind *needs* you to do.

It's called discipline, and it's really not that complicated. With two-year-olds, there are three important disciplinary goals:

- First, you want to set limits that contain your child's behavior but that do not interfere with the growth of mastery (competence).
- Second, you want to help your child develop the ability to delay gratification and tolerate frustration (one and the same, really).

◆ Third, you want to convince your child that you control his world and are thus capable of providing for and protecting him under any and all circumstances. To convince a two-year-old of this, you must first demonstrate that you are in charge of him—that no matter how much he screams, you're the boss. Needless to say, in order for you to demonstrate to your two-year-old that you are in control, you must first be in control of yourself.

In the sections that follow, I'm going to put together the building blocks of an effective discipline plan for your toddler.

Managing Your Toddler's Environment

The proper discipline of a two-year-old begins with taking steps to reduce discipline problems as much as possible. Remember, you're setting disciplinary precedents at this stage, and the most important precedent is that discipline—in the corrective or punitive sense of the term—is not a constant, contentious theme in the parent–child relationship. With proper environmental management, you can all but eliminate a number of problems that are common to this age. Here are the keys to reaching that goal:

Childproofing

At the beginning of this chapter, remember the mother's description of her always-on-the-go, getting-into-everything toddler? His mother's plaintive description fits the typical, full-steam-ahead child of this age. The solution is proper environmental management, the centerpiece of which is childproofing.

Toddlers are intensely inquisitive beings. They want to know what things are, how they work, what they do, how they come apart, and what it takes to break them. Exploring and experimenting—otherwise known as getting into things—are the name of the game. There is no other way for a toddler to figure out his world. He doesn't have the words with which to ask the questions, so he acts them out. Every new discovery raises more questions than it answers, further stimulating the child's curiosity. The more the toddler finds out, the more he wants to know, and the more active and inquisitive he becomes.

As the child's interest in his environment expands, parents should appreciate and respond to his need to explore by providing an environment that is both stimulating and safe. The most economical way of doing this, as well as the most sensible, is by childproofing. Childproofing a home shouldn't take more than a few hours and generally costs very little. These days, baby stores even carry childproofing supplies such as doorknob covers and safety covers for electric outlets.

Begin by taking inventory, a room at a time, of dangerous or valuable things that are within your child's reach. Keep in mind that if he isn't yet climbing, he soon will be. Put childproof latches on cabinets (especially lower ones), childproof covers on electrical sockets, and sturdy gates across any open staircases.

At the same time, bring down to your child's level things he can touch, explore, and experiment with. Give him a cabinet of his own in the kitchen and stock it with things like wooden spoons, pots, empty thread spools, boxes, flexible straws, and any other simple things. Keep in mind that most simple things are fascinating to a toddler. If you do a good job, your child should be able to roam around the house with minimal supervision.

It never fails: When I explain the advantages of childproofing to parents of toddlers, someone will ask how a child learns to discriminate between what he can and can't touch if parents remove the "can't touch" stuff from reach, if not sight. This misses the point entirely. Parents who childproof are not giving in to their children; they are accommodating their children's need to exercise curiosity and thus strengthen their minds.

Parents who refuse to childproof, who view this issue of getting into things as a test of wills, end up frustrating themselves as well as their child, and tantrums will abound. Midway through your child's third year of life (thirty months, give or take), you can begin slowly restoring the home to its previous state. Introduce one valuable at a time and let your child know it's not a plaything. As long you don't introduce too many interesting things at once, your child will cooperate with the boundaries being set.

Here's a tip for parents of toddlers when a child of this age picks up something fragile, like a piece of valuable crystal: The child is almost certain to throw the item to the floor if an adult puts on a horrified expression, shouts "No! Give me that!," and moves rapidly and threateningly toward him with arms outstretched, hands open like menacing claws. Panic breeds panic. Instead, control your anxiety, stay in one spot, squat down so you're at eye level with the child, put a smile on your face, extend your hand palm up, and say, "Oooooh, how pretty! Will you put it in my hand so I can see, too?" If you do a good acting job, the child will smile in return and place the item gently in your palm. Let the child know this wasn't a trick by drawing him into your lap and examining the object together for a minute or so. Then, get up and say, "I'm going to put this up here so we can both look at it. Isn't it pretty?" This procedure satisfies the child's curiosity, saves money, and helps build a cooperative, rather than antagonistic, parent–child relationship.

Tele-no-vision

My mother called it the "boob tube" and "idiot box" for good reason. The best of all worlds for a toddler is a world in which no television exists to pacify his or her intellect and imagination. Of course, this means taking the all-but-unheard-of step of removing the television from the family room, if not the house. But if you simply can't comprehend a life without television for yourself, then record your programs and watch them after your child's asleep.

You may think television is doing you a favor by keeping your dervish from whirling while it's on, but you're sadly mistaken. Television watching prevents a child from learning to occupy his time creatively and constructively. Therefore, the more you use the television set to occupy your young one, the more likely it is that he's going to pester, pester, pester when it isn't on. The more you use television to free up time for yourself, the more dependent on the television he—and you—will become.

Besides, you want him to grow up with all the smarts he was born with, don't you? In order to activate those smarts and keep them activated, a child needs to be *active*. The more opportunity a toddler has to explore and experiment on the environment, the smarter he will become. My formula for a Smart Kid consists of what I call the Six Es of Excellence: *Expose* the child to *Environments* and *Experiences* that *Enable Exploration* and *Experimentation*. In that context, folks, television simply fails to cut the proverbial mustard. It produces an electronic environment that depresses exploration and experimentation. For proof of what I'm saying, simply watch a child watch television. See the blank expression? See the listless hands? See the lack of any creative, constructive behavior? You're looking at a child wasting precious creative time. At my age, I look for opportunities to rest my brain, but a toddler's brain craves stimulation—and the artificial, tasteless, odorless world of television just doesn't cut it.

The time between a child's birth and seventh birthday (some say sixth, some eighth, so seventh will do) are known as the *formative years*. These are the years during which the child's competency skills are in formation. These skills—verbal, perceptual–motor, intellectual, social, creative—are programmed into the human embryo at the moment of conception. From the moment of birth on, all that's needed to release that potential is generous exposure to environments and experiences that enable exploration and experimentation. That's right, those same Six Es of Excellence. The more the Six Es abound in a child's life, the more excellent, in every sense of the term, he or she will become.

In 1979, I wrote a newspaper article proposing that television was actually addictive. I further speculated that it shut down crucial areas of the brain and shortened a child's attention span. I was mocked by a number of other professionals and organizations that advocate for parents of children with attention deficit hyperactivity disorder. Since that time, several researchers have proven beyond a shadow of a doubt that I was right.

According to one study, gifted children watch an average of less than five hours of television a week during their preschool years. Compare that with a national average of twenty-five hours, and you can begin to appreciate what a drain on the brain the boob tube truly is. Furthermore, if less than five hours a week of television is good for the brain, then none is even better! Indeed, more and more developmental pediatricians are now recommending that preschool children watch no television.

Besides, if you childproof your home such that your child can explore and experiment to his or her heart's content, thus requiring little supervision, you will not have a toddler constantly pestering you to entertain him.

Toy Management

There are two kinds of toys: those that are store-bought and those the child improvises for himself. Most store-bought toys are fairly worthless for this age child. They tend to be one-dimensional—in other words, capable of being one thing and one thing only. A truck is a truck is a truck, period. Realistic toys offer a child little opportunity for truly creative, improvisational play.

Creative toys are capable of being more than one thing. The more things the toy can become, the more creative the toy. In this category, we find such toys as blocks, Legos, Tinker Toys, Lincoln Logs, crayons, and finger paints. Notice that all the aforementioned toys were in production before 1955. Since then, very few toys of creative value have been produced. Creative toys also include everyday household items I've already mentioned: empty boxes, wooden spoons, pots and pans, empty oatmeal containers, thread spools, pieces of scrap wood, string, and Mom's and Dad's old clothes.

These sorts of playthings help a child get in touch with what I call the Magical Make-Do of Childhood. Making do is the essence of resourcefulness, which is the essence of creativity. Making do is the ability to do a lot with a little. Making do is when you want to make a forest, so you go outside and gather pinecones. Each pinecone becomes a pine tree. Making do is when you want to put a house in the middle of your forest of pinecones, so you use a shoebox. Making do is when you want furniture for your shoebox house in your pinecone forest, so you use spools, stones, smaller boxes, and bottle caps.

A child doesn't learn to do a lot with a little if his parents gift him with a lot of store-bought toys. Too many toys overwhelm a child's ability to choose a plaything and keep himself occupied. Too many toys prevent the emergence of imaginative play. Too many toys make it all but impossible for a child to learn to make do. Invariably, a child who complains a great deal about being bored is one who's been given too much. He's unable to make creative sense of the clutter of toys in his environment.

"Yes," you say, "I'd love for my child to have nothing but empty boxes and the like to play with, but his grandparents buy him thing after thing after thing after thing. What am I to do?"

I have the solution to the grandparent problem, one that's not likely to make anyone upset. Tell doting grandparents you think it's wonderful that they want to do so much for their grandchild. But you think it best they keep the toys they buy at their house. That way, your child will always know that certain toys are gifts from his grandparents. In addition, the toys become more special, the grandparents become more special, and going to their house becomes more special. Hey! Who can argue with that?

I know, your child's grandparents will probably argue with it. In that case, as soon as they leave, spirit the toys away. Bring them out of hiding five minutes before their next visit. What they don't know won't upset them.

Effective Communication

For every two-year-old, there is a parent asking, "Is there some key, some secret, to getting my child to do what I tell him to do?"

The honest answer to the question is, "No, there is not *one* key that will reliably open the lock of obedience with this age child." But neither is there cause for despair, for there are ways to improve one's chances of getting cooperation.

Environmental management goes a long way toward reducing disciplinary problems, but in some cases not far enough. The healthiest home environment doesn't guarantee cooperation. You take the second step toward disciplinary nirvana through the three Cs of effective communication: *Concrete, Concise,* and *Commanding.*

Use Concrete Words

Don't say, "Mommy wants you to be a good boy while we're in the store, okay?" Instead, tell your little bull in the china shop of life exactly what you want him to do while in the store, and keep it simple. Don't rattle off a list of ten or even three dos and don'ts. How about one? Try, "While we're in the store, you must stay in your stroller."

"But," you might say, "I want him to keep his hands off things and not throw tantrums and be quiet while I'm talking to salespersons and not spit at people who stop to say 'hello' to him and . . ."

Yes, I know you want all those things, but he's only two. He can't remember all that. As a consequence, he will not cooperate with any of it. Expect him to remember just one thing, the most important thing. Once he's got that down pat, then add another expectation, and so on. Believe it or not, you'll make progress more quickly if you don't rush things.

Being concrete also means not using the word "don't." Two-year-olds have difficulty understanding exactly what "don't" means. It's a fairly sophisticated abstraction, referring to the absence of a certain action. So, for example, when you say, "Don't climb on the table," your two-year-old hears, "Gibberish climb on the table." So, wanting nothing more than to make you happy, he climbs on the table. You might instead simply say, "No" (not yelled, but with emphasis) and quickly remove him from the table. Or just "Get down."

Be Concise

Don't use fifty words when five will do. Besides, with this age child, if five won't do, then no amount will. Being concise also means not explaining yourself. Twos understand simple instructions but not explanations. Going back to the previous example, a two-year-old who's climbing on a table will understand a firm "Get off the table" but will not understand "Sweetie, you need to get down from the table because you could fall and hurt yourself, and we might have to take you to the doctor, and that would make Mommy sad because I don't like to see my little boy get hurt, okay?"

In this case, the child will only hear, "Gibberish table, gibberish fall, more gibberish doctor, blah, blah, Mommy, blah-blah-blah hurt." He'll think a table fell on the doctor and Mommy got hurt. So do yourself and your child a favor and keep it to "Get off the table." And yes, that's very abrupt, but it works. Find out for yourself.

Command, Not Demand

To command is the opposite of being wishy-washy. You are wishy-washy when you plead, bargain, bribe, or threaten. You are commanding when you preface what you want with either "I want" or "You must" or "It's time for you to" or something equally assertive. Instead of saying either "If you pick up these toys, I'll give you ice cream," or "If you don't pick up these toys, I'll [fill in some awful threat]," say "It's time for you to pick up your toys."

You might be asking, "What if I do that and my child just stands there and looks at me as if to say, 'Make me.' What do I do then?"

You wait for a *strategic opportunity*. In other words, instead of launching yourself impulsively into battle with your child, you leave the toys where they are, bide your time, and wait until your child wants something from you. Twenty minutes later, for instance, he asks you to read him a story. You take his hand, lead him over to the toys, and say, "Before Mommy can read you a story, you must pick up these toys." And he does. Maybe. Please keep in mind that there are no perfect solutions, just potential solutions that are better than others.

But I jump ahead of myself, because waiting for a strategic opportunity is but one example of *proactive* or *managerial* discipline, which we shall take up next.

An Ounce of Prevention

One of the most unfortunate of prevailing attitudes toward disciplining children is the emphasis placed on punishment. When a child misbehaves, parents aren't likely to ask, "What is the most appropriate response?" Instead they ask, "How should we punish?" That's unfortunate. Indeed, punishment is sometimes the most appropriate response to misbehavior, but with this age child, one has to keep one's options open. Management, not punishment, is the key. A managerial approach to discipline includes punishment, but that's not the whole story, and it shouldn't be even the biggest part of the story. A punitive approach to toddler discipline is potentially problematic in five ways:

Punishment is reactive. More often than not, it's a knee-jerk response to having the proverbial rug pulled out from underneath and is usually driven by a certain amount of frustration or anger. Management, on the other hand, is *proactive*. Its success depends on foresight and planning. And preparedness, as every Boy Scout knows, is the best way of keeping frustration under control.

Punishment is confrontational. The inevitable outcome is either win–lose or lose–lose, either of which is undesirable in the parent–child relationship. Ironically, whereas punishment may temporarily suppress a power struggle, it almost always sets the stage for a later one. In no time at all, parent and child become engaged in a vicious, circular game of who can outmaneuver the other.

Punishment is inconsistent. It's difficult, if not impossible, for a halfway sensitive parent to deliver punishment without feeling some measure of regret afterward. No one likes to feel bad, especially about herself, so *parents who punish are understandably inconsistent.* Inconsistency prevents a child from being able to anticipate the consequences of his or her behavior and make appropriate adjustments. A punitive approach to discipline not only promotes and prolongs testing but also prevents a child from learning self-control. Therefore, it is incompatible with the overall aim of discipline.

Punishment alone often creates the illusion that the "crime" has been paid for, that the child has no further debt. For example, consider a child who talks back to another adult and whose parents punish by spanking and keeping him indoors for the remainder of the day. That may deter future disrespect, but it fails to make the child accept full responsibility for his or her actions. A sound managerial approach would involve having the child make an unassisted apology to the offended adult.

A punitive approach to misbehavior often results in a parent–child power struggle. A properly executed managerial approach to discipline helps a child learn how to successfully manage himself. Self-discipline is intrinsically rewarding. Therefore, a managerial approach to discipline is unlikely to result in a power struggle between parent and child.

Proactivity is the primary, defining characteristic of a strategic, managerial approach to discipline. I refer to it as "striking while the iron is cold." This simply means that the most effective time for dealing with misbehavior is *before* it occurs.

Most of us have heard the expression, "Strike while the iron is *hot*." It means you should seize opportunity when it's first presented. It's another way of saying that in hesitation, all may be lost. Although striking while the iron is hot may apply well to certain situations, it does not apply well to the discipline of children. In fact, many valuable teaching opportunities are lost because parents tend to strike at disciplinary situations *only* when the iron is hot.

I am referring to cases in which a child misbehaves and parents react punitively, in anger and frustration. Within the framework of this sort of knee-jerk, *reactive* approach to discipline, the intended lesson is lost in a chaos of emotion. Because parents inadvertently fail to communicate their expectations clearly, the child continues making the same behavioral mistakes.

Proactive discipline, on the other hand, all but ensures that parents will respond to behavior problems with confidence and balance. Because their emotions are in check, the parents are able to communicate clearly, and the child is able to listen.

Proactive discipline is a three-step process:

1. Anticipate the problem, based on knowledge of your child or children in general.
2. Develop a strategy for dealing with the problem, before the problem occurs again. By the way, there are few *wrong* strategies. In the final analysis, what you do about a problem is

less important than knowing what you are going to do *before* the problem occurs.

3. Communicate your proactive decision to the child. You define the problem and describe your strategy. With a two-year-old, remember the importance of being concise, as in, "Today, if you run away from me in the park, I'm going to take you home." This is not a threat. Threats are emotionally driven and rarely followed through with. This is information. When the problem occurs, you implement your strategy, following through as often as necessary until the problem is resolved.

Proactivity is how you keep your cool when your child misbehaves. Remember that you already know the problem is going to happen. You've accepted it. When it occurs, you're not upset because you're prepared for it. You already know what you're going to do. Thus, proactive discipline all but ensures that when behavior problems arise, you will be able to respond with both feet planted firmly on the ground.

If you fail to be proactive, when disciplinary problems arise you will feel yourself being thrown off balance. As a result, you will react emotionally and therefore ineffectively.

For example, let's say you don't have any choice but to take your two-and-a-half-year-old along on a shopping trip. You know from experience that a tantrum is likely to occur in the store. You take a few moments to consider your options and decide what you're going to do when the all-but-inevitable tantrum begins.

In this case, you decide simply to take your child back to the car until the tantrum subsides. (I should mention, at this point, that with this age child, it's not always necessary that you communicate your strategy beforehand. Whether you do or don't is a judgment call from situation to situation.) When the tantrum begins, you simply pick your child up (holding him facing away from you, of course), saying, "No screaming in stores. We're going to the car, where you can scream all you want." And to the car you go.

Because you anticipated and planned for it, the tantrum doesn't take you by surprise. Because you don't feel upended, you are able to communicate a sense of confidence, of authority, to your child. As a result, your child is able to regain his own balance more quickly. Sound too good to be true? Try it, and discover for yourself.

In a situation of this sort, dry runs work extremely well. An example of a dry run would be going to a store when you don't need to go. The purpose is to teach your child a lesson when you're under no pressure. You go to the store, you pretend to be looking around, your child says he wants something, you tell him he can't have it, a tantrum ensues, and you promptly leave the store, put him in the car, and go home. And you're not inconvenienced at all! Two or three dry runs ought to do it.

Consequences, Pro and Con

One of the biggest words in the vocabulary of discipline is *consequences*. When a child misbehaves, people tend to think in terms of doing something to persuade the child that the misbehavior in question will not result in what's called a *payoff*. Consequences certainly have their place, but the emphasis put on them has blinded many people to other, equally effective means of dealing with behavior problems. Sometimes, consequences aren't necessary at all. Sometimes, as the following story illustrates, *cunning* is all it takes.

Some time ago, my wife and I were having lunch with a friend and her toddler. The child dropped his napkin on the floor, and his mother told him to pick it up. He gave her an infuriating look and did nothing. She told him again, more insistently. He just sat there. Finally, she gave up.

A few minutes later, we all heard an airplane flying overhead. Said toddler became very excited. I said, "Would you like to fly airplanes someday?" He nodded his head enthusiastically, and so

I followed up with, "Then you have to pick up your napkin." He promptly got down and picked up the napkin. After all, pilots must be obedient. That's another example of waiting for a *strategic opportunity*. Put another way, good things come to those who wait.

Consistency

Unless parents are consistent with their discipline, a child cannot predict consequences. That ability to predict consequences and adjust behavior accordingly is the essence of self-discipline. It follows, therefore, that a child cannot learn to discipline himself unless his parents first discipline him with consistency.

Any child can be counted on to test any rule. Testing is a child's way of discovering whether the rule truly exists. Telling the child "This is a rule" isn't convincing enough. Children—especially young ones—are concrete thinkers. Rules must be *demonstrated*. So when a child breaks a rule, parents have an obligation to impose some form of discipline. This gets the child's attention and says, "See? We were telling you the truth." Parents demonstrate their reliability by being consistent. The more a child knows he can rely on his parents, the more secure the child will feel.

On the other hand, if a child breaks a stated rule, and instead of *doing something assertive*, his parents threaten or talk themselves blue in the face or get excited but don't do anything, the child is forced to test the rule again. Testing of this sort spins the child's wheels. It wastes time and energy the child could otherwise use in creative, constructive activity. Consistency frees children from the burden of having to test rules repeatedly.

Many parents think that being consistent means administering the same discipline each and every time a child misbehaves in a certain manner. Not so. Consistency is more a matter of *attitude* than technique. In fact, it is unrealistic to suppose that you will always be able to deliver the same consequence every time a child misbehaves in a certain way. But you can always convey the same attitude. In other words, you can display your disapproval and do something as a demonstration that you are in control. The something you do doesn't have to be the same something from misbehavior to misbehavior. It just needs to be something that says, "I won't allow you to behave like that."

Say your two-year-old becomes disruptive while you have company. You take him to his crib and leave the room. He screams and shakes the sides of the crib for a minute or two. You go back to his room and, standing in his doorway, ask, "Are you ready to come out and play quietly with your toys?" He says he is, but in fact he still may need to test you a few more times before he's finally convinced you mean business.

The next day, he becomes disruptive in a restaurant. You take him outside, explaining to the manager as you go that you'll be back to finish your meal as soon as your pet beast quiets down. You take your "terrible" two-year-old to the car, put him in his car seat, and get behind the wheel. You then say, "When you stop screaming, we'll go back in the restaurant and finish our food." A minute later, he's still screaming. You turn around and say, "Are you ready to go back in and finish your lunch?" He says he is, but remember, he still may need to test you one or two more times.

You handled his disruptions at home and in the restaurant differently, yet similarly enough, and you were consistent from one situation to the next. Perhaps he becomes disruptive in a store a week hence. You had planned on buying him a new pair of shoes, but you say, "No shoes today," and take him home. He gets the message: You do not allow loud, attention-seeking behavior. Because of your consistency, he is eventually able to predict that when he is loud, you are going to do something that he won't like. But he doesn't know exactly *what* you're going to do. That's not important. What's important is he knows you're going to do *something*. As a result, he begins exercising more control over himself. He learns to discipline himself. And that's what it's all about!

Containment Versus Correction

Before we go any further and you get the feeling I'm leading you down the proverbial primrose path, I should tell you that it's not always possible to *correct* the behavior of a two-year-old. In other words, if your toddler has developed a certain undesirable behavior, you may just have to live with it until he's at least three. During this time you may have to accept that the behavior in question can only be *contained*. The good news is that a misbehavior that is properly contained can be easily corrected when the time comes.

Two-year-olds are impulsive. They don't think ahead, and they don't have much hindsight, either. As a result, it takes a great deal of persistence to get disciplinary messages across to them. For example, let's say your two-year-old refuses to take a nap. Not only do you think he needs one, but *you* need him to take a nap. He also refuses to stay in his bed at night, and putting him back in a crib isn't the answer because he can climb out of his crib. You've tried spanking him, but that only made him much more determined (as spankings often do with this age child). You've told him that if he doesn't stay in his room at naptime, you won't take him outside later. He doesn't seem to care. You've tried reasoning with him, explaining the benefits of sleep. Ha! Now what?

Now you must accept that you aren't going to be able to correct this problem until he's older. For now, you can only contain it. So you hire a handyman to cut your son's bedroom door in half. He re-hangs the bottom half only, making a Dutch door, and turns the lock around. Now, when you put your son in for a nap, you close his new half-door and lock it. He can't get out, but he can still see out. He gets mad, but he doesn't become terrified.

The first few times you do this, he screams bloody murder. He's not afraid, just mad as the dickens. Each time, you wait five or so minutes before going back to his room. You peer over his half-door and say, "Everything's all right. I'm in the living room reading a book. It's time for you to get into your bed and take a nap. I'm going back to the living room now." You walk away. He continues to scream. You wait a few minutes and do the same thing, and you keep going back to his room every few minutes until he's quiet, which may take an hour or more the first time you do this.

Does it matter whether he actually takes a nap? No. What matters is that he stays in his room for an hour, giving you some time to yourself. Eventually, he accepts being put in his room at naptime, accepts the fact he can't get out, and plays for ninety minutes. You haven't corrected the problem, but you've contained it. You've established boundaries around the problem, limiting it to manageable proportions. When he's three, you can tell him that if he comes out of his room before naptime is over, you won't take him outside later. At three, he can think ahead. So he listens and stays in his room. Now you can buy a new door.

The difference between correction and containment applies to many problems typical to the stage of development under discussion— tantrums, for example. When our daughter, Amy, was two, she began throwing wild tantrums over anything and everything that didn't go her way. We tried the usual approaches: spanking her and ignoring her. Neither worked. Finally, we came to our senses and realized we were fighting a losing battle. She wasn't going to stop throwing tantrums until she had developed a better tolerance for frustration. Until then, we could only contain her fits of pique. So, we childproofed the downstairs bathroom and presented it to her as her new "tantrum place."

"From now on, Amy," we told her, "every time you want to have a tantrum, we're going to put you in this special tantrum place, and you can have your tantrum here. We picked the bathroom because it has a carpet for you to roll around on, and if you scream so loudly that you have to go to the bathroom, you're already there!"

From that time on, every time Amy began to scream when things didn't go her way, we simply said, "You can only throw tantrums in your tantrum place, Amy," and took her to the bathroom as quickly as we could. As soon as we closed the door, she'd stop screaming. Nonetheless, she'd stay in there for a few minutes—fuming, we supposed—before emerging. Did this stop her from having tantrums? No, it only contained them to a certain area of the house. She continued to throw them until she was three, when they began tapering off.

The point I'm making is that if you try to eliminate an undesirable behavior with this age child, you may only frustrate yourself. Concentrate instead on containing it. Containment may be all that's realistically possible. In addition, the assertiveness and self-control you display in the course of containing the behavior will pay off handsomely when your child is old enough for you to begin actually correcting it.

Setting Proper Disciplinary Precedents

The disciplinary style you develop when your child is this age will be precedent setting. Therefore, it's important that the precedents you set be of long-term benefit to both you and your child. In all that I've said in this chapter, and in all I've yet to say, I'm trying to illustrate a disciplinary style that embodies the following elements:

- Management, as opposed to punishment (but proper management will include punishment at times)
- Proactivity, as opposed to reactivity

- Assertiveness, as opposed to anger
- Consistency, as opposed to unpredictability
- Good communication, as opposed to outbursts of emotion

If you succeed at incorporating these characteristics into your discipline at this stage of the game, then discipline should never become a big deal in your relationship with your child. A disciplinary style that embodies these elements is one that fosters self-discipline. And the earlier and better your child disciplines himself, the more joy there will be in your parenthood, and because obedient kids are happy kids, the happier his childhood will be. Furthermore, by properly disciplining your child now, you take out an insurance policy that greatly reduces the possibility of later behavior problems.

I once counseled a family in which the problem child was a sixteen-year-old whom I will call Lynnette. Over the two years before I saw the family, Lynnette had become extremely rebellious. She took every possible opportunity to "sneak around," as her parents put it. She associated with kids her parents disapproved of, went places her parents told her she was not to go, and did things her parents forbade, like drinking and smoking.

One of the stories her parents told was especially interesting. Almost every time Lynnette went somewhere in the family car, she brought back empty beer cans in the back seat or half-smoked marijuana cigarettes in the ashtray. It was as if she was openly flaunting her disregard of her parents' rules. When her parents confronted her with the evidence, Lynnette would deny knowing anything about it. She'd claim that one of her friends had put the beer cans in the back seat without her knowledge, that someone to whom she gave a ride had left the joint in the ashtray. Her parents could never get her to admit to any wrongdoing.

One day, Lynnette's parents were especially frustrated. During their visit, her mother said, "I knew when Lynnette was two that she was going to be a permanent headache."

"How's that?" I asked.

It seems that when Lynnette was two, she would hold her bowel movements by squeezing her legs together. When asked whether she had to go to the bathroom, she would insist that she didn't. Later, her parents would find a bowel movement in a corner of the living room or, one time, in a shoebox in their bedroom closet.

"I'd ask her if she had made the b.m.," her mother said, "and she'd always deny it. I could never get her to admit that she was the one who'd left the poop for me to clean up."

I immediately realized that the precedent her parents had set when Lynnette was two years old was still operating in their relationship. At two, she pooped in the corner and denied it. At sixteen, she (figuratively speaking, of course) "pooped" in the family car and denied it. Things hadn't changed in fourteen years. And not with Lynnette alone. When she was two and she pooped in a corner or a shoebox, her parents had reacted emotionally. Even though mis-pooping occurred over and over again, the parents never stepped back, took a deep breath, and developed a plan of action. Every time it happened was like the first time—her parents got all up in arms, yelled, stomped around, threatened, but did nothing. And sure enough, the same thing was still going on now that Lynnette was sixteen. She "pooped" in the family car, and her parents got all up in arms, yelled, stomped around, threatened, but did nothing.

I've made the same observation time and time again in the course of counseling families. For better or worse, the themes that characterize the parent–child relationship when the child is two are the same themes that characterize the relationship later, especially during the child's early and middle teen years. A smooth relationship at two predicts a smooth relationship at fourteen. On the other hand, a rocky relationship at two predicts the same at fourteen.

So, get your disciplinary act together now, and you may never have to get it together again!

Biting Off No More
Than You Can Chew

Good discipline doesn't have to be complicated. Rather, it must be well organized, easily communicated, and easily dispensed. The simpler, the better.

Another way of dooming discipline to failure is to bite off more than you can chew. Let's take, for example, a child who's destructive, disobedient, irresponsible, unmotivated, aggressive, disrespectful, and loud. Instead of tackling all the problems at once, which would be like wrestling with an octopus, it would be better to concentrate on just one—the easiest one. Solving one problem puts you in a good position to solve another, and then another, and so on.

The parents of two children, ages four and two, were having the usual problems that come with having two preschoolers. They sassed, squabbled, screamed, jumped on furniture, wrote on the walls, ran through the house, got into everything, and created general bedlam. The parents raced from one child to the other, one thing to the next, driving themselves bananas in the process. They reminded me of the plate-spinners I used to see on *The Ed Sullivan Show*. The more they tried to accomplish, the less they accomplished.

"Pick two problems," I told them.

They picked sassing and screaming. Neither child could read, so we drew pictures, one for each problem. Screaming was represented by a stick-child with mouth wide open, sassing by a stick-child sticking a stick-tongue out at a stick-parent. Artists we weren't.

The pictures were posted on the refrigerator, and the children were told what each of them meant. The parents bought a timer and kept it handy to the children's rooms. When one of the targeted misbehaviors occurred, the parent closest at hand would identify the behavior ("That's sassing") and say, "That's one of your pictures and means you have to spend ten minutes in your room." The parent would take the offending child to his or her room, set the timer for ten minutes, and walk away. When the bell rang, the children came out of their neutral corners.

I stressed the importance of adhering to the referee's rule: No threats, no second chances, no deals. "When an infraction occurs," I said, speaking figuratively, "blow the whistle and assess the penalty. And remember that in hesitation, indecision, or negotiation, all is lost."

I saw them again three weeks later. Mom started off by telling me she had finally found a whistle at a sporting goods store. I was incredulous.

"You mean you actually went out and bought a real referee's whistle?"

"Sure did," Mom replied. "It sounded like a good idea to me. When we're home, I wear it around my neck. If I blow the whistle, the kids march to their rooms. I don't even have to tell them to go. Better yet, they've learned to set the timer themselves."

I asked how she felt about the plan, and here's what she told me, word for word: "I feel more confident in my parenting skills, and more in control of my children. The children are reacting in a way that tells me they're more confident of my authority. They've learned my limits. Before, we were at the point of constant frenzy. Now the household is calm. It's a very organized feeling, and everyone is happier!"

Strike another blow for simplicity.

Those Four Bad Words

Over the years, I've received my share of letters from people chastising me for giving parents permission to say, "Because I said so." They all say the same thing: "Children need to know the reasons behind the decisions parents make."

No, they don't. Any more than an infantryman needs to know why his commanding officer gave the order he gave. The military isn't a democracy, and neither is a family. "Because I said so" is nothing but a declaration of parent authority. As such, it should be clearly stated, not shouted at a child.

Explanations invite argument, and arguments between parent and child are decidedly nonproductive. They go nowhere. The notion that children need to know the reasons behind their parents' decisions implies that children can understand those reasons. They can't. The proof of this is that they never agree with them. No child has ever said, "Well, you know, Mom, now that you've explained yourself so well, I can't help but agree with you about this. Yes, I was wrong." The incontrovertible fact is that if a child doesn't like a decision his parents make, he won't like the reason behind the decision either. Therefore, "Because I said so" is the only explanation a child needs.

Now, hear me clearly: *I'm not saying that parents should never give reasons to children.* I'm saying parents should make no attempt to *reason with* children, and the difference is night and day. Reasoning is the futile attempt to persuade a child that your point of view is valid. Face it, children will understand an adult point of view when they are adults, and no sooner. No amount of words will instill an appreciation for an adult point of view into the mind of a child.

If you want to explain yourself, then by all means do so. But don't expect your child to agree. When he doesn't, simply say, "I'm not asking you to agree. I wouldn't agree with me either if I were your age. As I've told you before, you are free to disagree, but you are not free to disobey."

In other words, the child does what he is told not because you succeed at providing an explanation that satisfied him but simply because you told him. Period. So even in the act of giving reasons, the bottom line is still, "Because I said so."

Questions?

Q *Several weeks ago, our eighteen-month-old son had a bowel movement while we were giving him a bath. We were all somewhat surprised, but Josh was downright frightened. Since then, when it comes time for his bath, he climbs into the tub but refuses to sit down. If we attempt to force him, he stiffens and goes into hysterics. Several times, he has promised us he's going to sit, but once in the tub, he changes his mind. We've talked reassuringly about the accident. The talks go fine, but nothing changes. This may not sound like a big problem, but it's got us at our wits' end. Do you have any suggestions?*

A Sounds like your typical toddler–parent standoff: He won't sit for it, and you won't stand for it.

Let's review the situation: Josh is in the tub splashing water all over everyone, blowing bubbles, giggling, when suddenly, what's this? Oh, my goodness, Dr. Spock never told us this would happen. Josh doesn't understand what's going on, but he can tell by the looks on your faces that whatever it is, it isn't good. So he moves fast to get out, and you move fast to get him out. The next time you announce a bath, Josh faces a dilemma. He likes the tub, but he doesn't like what happened the last time he was there, and he's sure as heck not going to put himself in that same position again.

"I'll just stand, thank you."

"No, you'll sit."

"No, I'll stand!"

"Sit!"

"Stand!"

Haven't you heard? Toddlers have minds of their own. Strong ones, too. In fact, extensive laboratory research has determined that the mind of the average toddler is stronger by 1.5 quantities than the average adult biceps, so the more you pull, the more-and-a-half Josh pushes. Meanwhile, the issue gets big, then bigger, then biggest. The bigger the issue, the stronger his will and the weaker, by comparison, your bicep.

Forget reasoning with Josh. He's on to your tricks. The fancy words, the soothing tone, all designed to lull him into a sense of false security. Josh (to himself): "They think I'm dumb. Watch this."

> *Parents:* "Josh, listen, the other day you pooped in the tub and blah, blah, blah, it was just an accident and blah, blah, blah, it's dangerous to stand and blah, blah, and furthermore blah, blah, you understand, don't you, sweetheart?"
>
> *Josh (nodding convincingly):* "Uh-huh."
>
> *Parents:* "Good! Then sit down."
>
> *Josh:* "Nope. Stand."

Nice try, folks. Back to the drawing board.

Instead of trying to meet Josh's willpower head on, instead of trying to convince him there's nothing to worry about, offer him a strategic compromise. That's where you get him to do what you want, but make it seem like it was all his idea. It's rumored that wives often do this with their husbands.

A strategic compromise is parent-judo. In this case, you need to make Josh an offer that appears to compromise your position but doesn't compromise either your authority or Josh's autonomy. It's easier than it may sound.

Being proactive, before Josh's next bath, you say, "Josh, you don't have to sit in the tub tonight, but you can't stand, either, because you might fall down. So, you have to kneel, like this."

Demonstrate what you're talking about and have him practice a few times, praising him for his excellent kneeling. Once he's mastered the technique, take him to the tub.

Now you've got him. Once Josh experiences the "joys" of kneeling, he's going to want to find a more comfortable position. But you told him he can't stand, so what's left? You've got it! Problem solved!

Q *Over the last few months, Sam, our twenty-month-old son, has developed the disturbing habit of violently banging his head on a hard surface, like the floor, when he's frustrated. I've tried teaching him alternative ways of expressing his feelings, such as foot stomping, but with no success. As a result, he has a constantly bruised forehead. A child psychologist I talked with told me to ignore it, but I'm afraid he will hurt himself if I do. When he starts banging I stop him, at which point he struggles with me. This happens several times a day. Other than this, he's a cheerful little guy. I believe this is a phase, but I was hoping you might have a way of bringing it to a quick end.*

A You're absolutely right. Sam will eventually stop banging his head. But if you do the right thing, he'll stop sooner than he would have otherwise. Contrary to the psychologist's advice, ignoring it is the wrong thing to do. Not only will Sam's head banging not go away if you ignore it, but it causes you too much anxiety to ignore. Besides, he could conceivably cause himself injury if you don't put some limits on the behavior. That means a trip to the emergency room and having to answer questions from people who think you may have caused the injury.

Before we go any further, let's get one thing straight: You can no more prevent him from banging his head than you can prevent him from throwing a tantrum. If he wants to throw a tantrum he's going to, and if he wants to bang his head he's going to.

Toddlers have reputations for reacting to frustration by doing bizarre things like banging their heads, biting themselves, and pulling out their hair—the kinds of aberrant behavior we associate with the inmates of an eighteenth-century insane asylum. No need to worry, however; it's all normal for the age. Toddlers bang their heads and bite themselves and throw themselves around because they're uncivilized. They continue to do things of this sort because of the attention these behaviors bring. The trick, then, is to come up with a way of not giving Sam attention for head banging without ignoring it.

There's a way of doing just that. It's a bit out of the ordinary, but every time I have recommended it, it's worked. First, find a section of blank wall in some out-of-the-way yet accessible part of the house. Using a washable crayon, draw a 2-foot-diameter circle on the wall, positioning the center at the height of Sam's forehead. Make sure that any wall studs are off to the side of the circle rather than dead center. Show Sam the circle and tell him that this is his very own head-banging place. Whenever he wants to bang his head, he should go there and bang because this is the best place in the whole world for that kind of thing.

Since you've also been teaching him to stomp his feet, you can draw a circle on the floor, directly beneath the head-banging circle, and tell him it's his very own special foot-stomping place. Now he can bang his head and stomp his foot at the same time, which is bound to help his coordination, if nothing else. Demonstrate how convenient it will be for him to bang his head in the special place by getting down on your knees and banging your own head a few times. Tell him how good it felt and encourage him to give a try.

Yes, I know this sounds strange, but it's kind of like fighting fire with fire. Sam will look at you like you've lost your marbles, and the next time he gets mad he will start banging his head in just any old place. When that happens, pick him up and take him to the special circle. Say, "Bang here in your special place!" and walk away.

If you do this every time he bangs his head, head banging should begin to taper off in a week or so. There's no future in banging your head unless your parents get upset over it. Within a month, it should be a thing of the past. Then he'll probably start biting himself, in which case you draw a circle on his forearm and . . .

Q *When I call my two-year-old daughter to come to me, she takes off running. She obviously thinks it's a game because she laughs as I chase her around. She's very quick and often hides in small places where I have difficulty going. I have spanked her for doing this, but that doesn't seem to have any lasting effect. What's a mother to do?*

A Well, of course it's a game! In fact, it's a combination of two of the oldest games in the books, invented long before there were books: "It" and "Hide-and-Go-Seek." Your daughter has no idea that this isn't as fun for you as it is for her, not until you get all worked up and pop her behind, that is. But as you've discovered, with this age child the effect of a spanking lasts about thirty seconds, after which it's off to the races again.

Think strategically. This particular game begins with you telling your daughter to come to you. As much as you want her to listen and obey, I'm afraid you're going to have to settle for less, for the time being at least. The solution is quite simple, really: Instead of telling her to come to you, simply walk over and take her by the hand or pick her up before she realizes what you're doing. As you're doing so, say, "Come with me."

Then, praise her for doing what you've told her to do. Just a simple "Good girl" will do.

"What?" you exclaim, incredulously. "But she didn't do anything!"

True, but remember, this is all about strategy, not logic. By acting like she has in fact obeyed you, you move closer to the day when she does begin obeying you. Eventually, you'll find that you can simply get within arm's reach of her, hold out your hand, and say, "Come with me," and she will cooperatively take your hand. With time, and equal patience, this problem will be solved.

One thing is for sure: The moment she takes off running, the game is on, and you've already lost. "Winning" will be a matter of smarter, not faster.

Q *I am the besieged parent of a two-year-old. Our pediatrician has recommended that when our daughter misbehaves, we make her sit in a chair for two minutes. It sounds good, but my daughter won't sit there. As soon as I begin to walk away, she gets up and follows me. The doctor told me to train her by setting a timer for two minutes and sitting with her until the bell rings. I tried this for about four weeks and got nowhere. Besides, I had to entertain her for the entire two minutes, which seemed to defeat the purpose of the discipline. Now the pediatrician is telling me to hold her in the chair, which doesn't appeal to me at all. Do you have any ideas?*

A First let me say that I agree with your feelings about sitting with her until the bell rings. I also agree that holding her in the chair for two minutes is not a good idea at all. It will only provoke a struggle and lots of screaming, serving only to replace one problem with another and setting the stage for escalating conflict in your relationship.

You can reasonably expect a three-year-old to sit in time-out for two or three minutes, but a younger child, as you've discovered, isn't likely to cooperate in sitting for a specific length of time. The good news is that whether a two-year-old sits or not isn't that important. What's important is that you respond assertively to the problem behavior, whatever it is.

When your daughter misbehaves—say she jumps on the living room sofa—you should first reprimand her ("No jumping!"); second, spell out the consequences ("I'm taking you to the no-no chair"); next, take her to the designated place (it can be any chair in the house, but it should be somewhere off by itself), put her in it, and say, "You're going to sit here until I tell you to get up." Then, take one step back and say, "Okay, you can get up now."

No doubt your daughter will begin getting up as soon as you step back. By giving her immediate permission to get up, you make it appear as if she's cooperating with you. Clever, eh? More important, you'll demonstrate that you are in control of yourself and her as well and that what you say goes. In the final analysis your *assertiveness* is what counts, not that she cooperates in sitting for a certain length of time.

If you do this consistently, within a couple of weeks your daughter will begin waiting for your signal before getting out of the chair. At that point, you can begin delaying permission to get up until she's sitting for fifteen seconds or so, which is quite long enough for this age child. Teaching her to wait for your signal prepares her for the day when you'll begin using a timer, which you can introduce when she's about three.

Q *I started using the time-out method you recommend with two-year-olds* [see the above question-and-answer], *and things are already going more smoothly between my thirty-month-old son and me. He still won't do what he's told, however. I tell him to pick up his toys, and he tells me he's not going to. I put him in the "no-no chair," take several steps away, and tell him he can get up. Then I again tell him to pick up his toys, and he again refuses. Do I put him back in the chair? That could go on all day.*

A Yes, that could go on all day, and no, you wouldn't accomplish anything by putting him back in the "no-no chair" except creating a power struggle. No one wins a power struggle. Besides, because this stage of development sets many precedents, power struggles now will only mean more power struggles to come. As I've already pointed out, there are no magic solutions to the disciplinary dilemmas parents encounter with two-year-olds. If a three-year-old won't pick up his toys, you can tell him he's not going outside later. He knows what "later" means, and he cares whether he goes outside or not. A two-year-old, on the other hand, couldn't care less about *later*. He cares only about right now, and the important thing right now is he's not going to pick up his toys. So there!

Ah, but if you are patient, a strategic opportunity will eventually present itself. Say you want him to pick up his toys, and he refuses. Just shrug your shoulders and walk away, leaving the toys on the floor. Later, when he wants to go outside or wants you to read him a book, take him by the hand, lead him back to the scene of the "crime," and say, "When you pick up these toys I'll take you outside."

At this point, if he's a normal two-year-old, he'll fall on the floor and start thrashing about while screaming at the top of his lungs. Just smile and tell him, "It's okay to scream. When you finish screaming, pick up the toys, and we'll go outside."

Needless to say, two-year-olds are extremely persistent little people. They can hold out for a long, long time. That's why it's important to wait patiently for a suitable strategic opportunity and resolve to hold out even longer. This is a nonpunitive way of asserting your authority that is emotionally cost-effective and keeps you out of power struggles. Once your son realizes you hold the key to the things he wants to do, he'll begin cooperating.

Q *When I ask him to do something, my two-year-old screams "No!" and then swings at me. When he hits me, I firmly reprimand him and try to put him in time-out, but that only makes matters worse. I've tried ignoring his screaming, but that doesn't work. What should I do?*

A The kind of behavior you describe—illogical, irrational, violent—has given many children well-deserved bad reputations at this age. It's also why one of my graduate school psychology professors maintained that toddlers were psychotic.

I could have told you that time-out wasn't going to work. And as for ignoring this kind of behavior, I don't know anyone who has that level of fortitude. Besides, the terrible two-year-old won't tolerate being ignored. It drives him into a frenzy.

But I have the solution. At least, it's worked for numerous other parents of equally psychotic toddlers. Try the Dutch door solution described on page 95 of this chapter. When your son screams, attempts to hit, or begins to show any other symptoms of imminent psychosis, pick him up, put him in his room, close the half-door, and lock it. Then walk away. Let him vent for as long as he needs to vent in order to realize that his bedroom is now his venting place—his only venting place. When he is calm, or reasonably so, go back, unlock the door, pull it open, and walk away. Don't say things like "Are you ready to be good?" or anything equally counterproductive. Act as if nothing has happened between picking him up and opening his door.

The key to the success of this tried-and-true method is to get him to his room as quickly as possible after an episode begins. In fact, if you even see him warming up for an episode, take him to his room. Do this for two weeks. If my experience serves me well, that's how long it will take for him to get it.

Two more things: First, keep it simple. When it comes to giving instructions to your son, don't ask; tell. There's a world of difference between "It's time for you to pick up your toys" and "How about being a good boy and picking these toys up for Mommy, okay?" Toddlers respond much more cooperatively to declarations than to requests. Second, make it easy. Don't give a toddler more than two toys to play with at once. That simplifies the job of picking them up and makes screaming a lot less likely. See my suggestion on page 49 for a toy lending library.

Q *Our first child is a month from being two. We're concerned about his throwing. During a recent dinner out, he threw a fork that whizzed by a lady's head, just missing her eye. I took a building block to the lip the other day, and Grandma got a metal car on the forehead. The articles I've read just say throwing is a way of exploring cause–effect relationships. We've tried consistent time-outs, redirecting, ignoring, and getting down to his level and telling him "No!" His throwing just keeps getting worse. He starts school in August, and I'm anticipating a lot of incident reports. Any suggestions?*

A My first bit of advice is that until the aerial assaults stop, you should keep your son out of places where he can pick up solid objects and wing them at unsuspecting strangers. In that event, the cause–effect just might be the following: injury–lawyers. (To be perfectly clear, I don't think toddlers should be allowed in restaurants that have waitstaffs even if they don't throw things.)

Yes, two-year-olds are known for throwing things. And yes, throwing is a way of exploring cause and effect, but the most immediate and fascinating effect in this case is that everyone gets upset. That's the payoff.

You tell me you've tried time-outs, but then you tell me you've also tried several other consequences, including ignoring. I am moved to point out that trying lots of different consequences is not consistent. When he throws something or even acts like he's thinking about throwing something, you need to put him in his room and gate him in there for at least ten minutes. If he's too strong for a gate, then try the Dutch door method described earlier.

When you put him in his room, you must do so without the slightest show of emotion, as if you're just following a formula. You needn't even say "No!" He's a smart kid, I'll wager. He'll get the message. If he screams for the entire fifteen minutes, so be it. The experience will not scar him, I assure you, but it will make an impression, however slowly.

When his time is up, just let him out. Don't lecture him or try to make him confess or apologize. Just let him out and go on your merry way, prepared to do the same thing the next time an incident occurs. Consistently done, this will cure his throwing in no more than four weeks. Even then, no restaurants for another two years. After all, I might be in the next one you take him to.

Q *My two-year-old daughter eats a few bites of supper each night and then wants milk. So I give her milk. Then she refuses to eat anything else. We take the milk away and attempt to bribe her to take a bite of this or a bite of that. Sometimes we make her something else to eat, something we know she likes. What can we do to get her to eat without hassles? I know that giving her milk before she's finished everything on her plate makes no sense, but I'm afraid that if I don't, it may lead to future eating problems.*

A The worry that not giving your daughter milk when she asks for it may eventually cause her to develop an eating disorder is a prime example of what I call a psychological boogeyman: an unfounded fear that paralyzes a parent's ability to think clearly about an issue and hence his or her ability to act effectively. You're hardly alone in this regard. I estimate that at least

90 percent of America's parents (mothers, mostly) are infected with one or more of these diabolical psychological viruses.

You're making a mountain out of an anthill. Wouldn't everyone's lives be simpler and therefore happier if you simply give your daughter milk when she wanted milk? If your daughter were not thriving, she would be symptomatic: dark half-circles under her eyes, lethargy, a distended tummy, and so on. In the absence of these symptoms, one is forced to conclude that nutrition is not a problem. Some toddlers eat like small horses, some eat like birds (a bad analogy, since most birds eat huge amounts of food relative to their body weights). In either case, these toddlers thrive. Milk is full of good vitamins. If you want to add some insurance into the equation, give her a chewable multivitamin every day.

Problems of this sort reinforce my belief that very young children should not be sitting at the grownups' table for family meals. The arrangement motivates parents to cajole a child to eat, and when that fails, they have to attempt force. The child becomes the focus of everyone's attention at the table and learns that she can manipulate her parents by refusing to eat what they want her to eat. The learning in question takes place intuitively, not consciously, but the end result is the same: family meals that are not pleasant for anyone.

Put a plate of bite-size fruits and veggies (carrot sticks, cucumber slices, orange wedges, dehydrated apple slices, and so on) out for your daughter to snack on during the day. Thirty minutes before you and your husband sit down to eat, put your daughter at the table (or a smaller, child-size table, which kids generally love) with her dinner. Let her eat what she feels like eating, then give her milk, then let her down, at which point you and your husband sit down to a peaceful, child-free conversation. When she's older and has developed a more ecumenical palate, have her join you. In the meantime, enjoy!

Q *Our two-year-old occasionally bites himself when he's angry, usually because he didn't get his way. Does this mean he's insecure or that something is troubling him emotionally? In any case, what can we do to stop him?*

A It's a whole lot easier to cure a toddler of biting other people than it is to prevent him from biting himself. As you already know, you can rarely predict when it's going to happen, and even if you do, you can't move fast enough to stop it. Typically, parents become alarmed and confused by a child's self-biting and generally respond with one form or another of uncivilized panic. They shriek, run for help, struggle to separate "Jaws" from his arm, or faint. They're also likely to think they have caused the child to bite himself by being bad parents. They feel guilty, and the child ends up being held and pampered. As a consequence of all this drama and attention, the child begins to bite himself more and more often, and before you know it, a mountain has been manufactured out of a molehill. When your toddler bites himself, do nothing. Pretend to be busy with something else. If he shows you the bite, tell him (matter-of-factly) how sorry you are that he hurt himself and go back to what you were doing. If he breaks the skin, calmly help him wash and apply antiseptic. If there's any doubt as to whether he's adequately protected against infection, call his pediatrician.

There are two answers to your question about possible insecurity. No, self-biting doesn't mean your son is insecure or psychologically damaged. Yes, something is troubling him emotionally: He didn't get his way about something. Such is life. Some toddlers teethe on themselves, usually out of frustration. When they get a dramatic reaction, they figure that biting themselves is a big deal and do it all the more. In an older child, persistent self-biting may be indicative of a psychological disturbance. But in a toddler, the occasional chomp on one's own arm is just one of those things.

Q *What is the best approach to handling unwanted behavior from my thirteen-month-old? For example, one thing she likes to do is shake the dining room chairs. She pulled one over on herself once, but that didn't stop it. Now, when she shakes the chairs, I tell her "No!" and put her in her playpen for about one minute. The bad behavior has since decreased. Is this type of punishment okay for a child this age, or should I just take the chairs out of the dining room until she's older?*

A A stern reprimand followed by a brief period of time-out is certainly appropriate punishment for a young toddler—when the misbehavior is not serious, as this is not. If you want to strengthen the message a bit, you might leave her in her playpen for two or three minutes, but longer than three is probably overkill. Don't expect quick results, however. Be as consistent as possible and be patient. If your daughter is slowly tearing the dining room chairs apart, it's probably advisable that you put them out of reach, but if the only problems are the noise and the chance she'll pull one over on herself again, I'd leave them where they are. Actually, having a chair topple over on her—unless the chairs are especially heavy—isn't threatening to life or limb and will probably cure this faster than a combination of "No!" and time-out in the playpen.

Q *I have a friend who puts her twenty-eight-month-old son in his room for several hours if he does something really bad, such as bite her. When he's there, he cries for a while, then he plays. She uses a gate so he can see out, but still, isn't this a bit much for a child this age? Can it be harmful?*

A A consequence will serve as an effective deterrent of inappropriate behavior only if it implants a permanent memory that the child can reliably associate with the offense in question. Generally speaking, brain development does not support long-term memory until around three. Therefore, it's likely that after five or ten minutes in his room, this child has completely forgotten why his mother put him there. So although I don't think that occasionally (the operative word) confining a two-year-old to his room for several hours is necessarily harmful, it is most definitely overkill. The most effective consequence to use with a toddler is three to five minutes of time-out. Since your typical two-year-old won't sit in a chair for longer than a few seconds, I recommend using a playpen, as long as it isn't used for anything but time-outs. For even a brief period of confinement to be effective at this age, it's important that as the parent releases the child, she must get him to say or remind him why he was confined in the first place.

Q *Our two girls, ages three and two, are very well behaved both at home and in public, so my husband and I decided to treat them to a memorable vacation at Disney World. As soon as we got through the gates, the girls became possessed by demons, and it turned out to be the most nightmarish four days we have ever had. One night they did not sleep until 2:30 a.m. I do not make threats I cannot follow through with, but I found myself saying things like, "We won't go into the park to see Cinderella tomorrow if you don't lie down and go to sleep." Needless to say, they still wouldn't sleep, and we weren't about to blow off the tickets. Because the girls were exhausted from not going to bed until midnight, we had tantrum after tantrum. Now my extended family wants to hold a reunion there this coming holiday season. Is there a discipline plan I can put in place now that will prevent another Disney Disaster?*

A Four days at Dizzy World with a three-year old and a two-year-old? What were you thinking? And what's this about treating them to a memorable vacation? The fact is, the older one may retain some vague memories of this experience, but the two-year-old forgot it within a week.

My recommendation, based on personal experience: I sincerely suggest that you and your children forgo the Disney World reunion, with appropriate excuses. Don't take a child to Disney World until he's at least six, and even then not if he's the least bit hard to handle in public places. Willie and I didn't take our kids until they were thirteen and nine. We had a truly wonderful time, and we all have wonderful memories. In fact, our kids actually liked Epcot more than they did the Magic Kingdom, where they quickly tired of standing in long lines.

Q *My two-year-old has a bad habit of purposely tipping over a regular cup at meals. He will take a drink and then just dump the rest onto the tray of his high chair. We have tried giving him a drink only when he asks, putting only a small amount of liquid in the cup at a time, and taking the cup away and not letting him have any more. None of that has helped. He still does this almost every meal. I have tried to not make a big deal out of it and just wipe it up or make him wipe it up, but he persists. Any advice?*

A I am convinced that many, if not all, of the mealtime problems today's parents are experiencing with toddlers are due to the latest practice of having infants and toddlers join the rest of the family for meals. This does nothing but provide them with a platform and audience for their shenanigans. It also causes meals to be tense experiences for parents and older siblings. As recently as the 1950s, very young children were fed separately, before the rest of the family sat down to eat. For example, I didn't eat with the adults until I was at least four, and I didn't suffer. I preferred it, in fact. I believe in feeding a young child first, and then having the rest of the family sit down to eat while the toddler is allowed to run around doing his own thing. When the high chair has served its purpose, buy a toddler-size table and chairs and put an absorbent pad under the table (these can be purchased at pet supply stores). Give your son very little liquid in the cup and let him have his fun. When he discovers he's no longer getting a reaction, this too will pass. Later, when he's amenable to being taught manners, let him come to the table, but until he can behave himself at family meals, keep the toddler table in reserve and use it at a moment's notice.

Q *Our sixteen-month-old son refuses to feed himself. He will not even touch his food other than to throw it to the floor. If I try to put a bit of finger food in his hand, he acts like I'm burning him. As a result, I have to feed him every bite, and he is becoming more and more picky about what he will eat. He even refuses to use a sippy cup or hold his own bottle, so I still hold it for him. Most recently, he's started acting afraid of sitting in his high chair. Should we try a different type of chair?*

A This is yet another problem caused by letting infants and young toddlers sit at the grownups' table. My advice is that parents feed an infant separately, not during the family meal. While you are feeding the child, do other things, so your focus is not entirely on him. Feed him a bite, then get up and do something else, then come back and feed another bite, and so on. As soon as possible, introduce finger foods so the child gets used to self-feeding. Pay no attention to how much he eats. Don't encourage or entice or act like a cheerleader. Finally, when he seems done, let him down. Whether a baby eats a lot or a little, he will satisfy his hunger.

Now, here's how to uncreate your family food monster: To begin, stop feeding him. Leave a platter of finger food and a sippy cup out, all day long, at his level. Let him graze. You and your husband should eat by yourselves as he wanders around. Don't invite him to the table, and if he comes over and asks for food, direct him to his finger foods. Pay absolutely no attention to what he eats or how often or how much. In addition, make the bottles disappear. When he asks for one, just say, "No more bottle" and direct him to his sippy. It may take as much as a day, but he will begin drinking.

After giving this same advice to another mother who was having the same problem with her young toddler, she wrote me back, saying, "We followed your instructions, and they worked perfectly! It was quite difficult when he was trying to hand me a bit of finger food, sobbing, and saying 'Ma-ma, Ma-ma,' but we held firm, and he's now feeding himself. He's obviously quite proud of himself as well."

To the folks who think infants should get used to eating with the rest of the family, I say there's a time for everything, and this age is not the time. Even if a child does not eat with the family until age four, he will civilize quickly. Besides, that's four years of invaluable mealtime peace.

Q *My two-year-old son attends a toddler program three mornings a week, and my friend and I take turns carpooling to the center. Last Monday, when she arrived at our house, Iggy suddenly announced he wasn't going with her. When I asked him why not, he screamed, "I don't want to!" After a struggle, I gave up and drove him myself. The same thing happened the next two times it was my friend's turn to drive. She suggested I just hand him over and let her handle it, but I don't want to push a screaming two-year-old off on anyone else. I talked to him*

about it, and he promised to ride with her later, but not now.
Can you explain his sudden change in behavior?

A Iggy has already told you why he doesn't want to ride with your
friend. He doesn't want to! Two-year-olds don't know why they
do things. They just decide to do something, then they do it.
Why? Because.

You must stop talking so much. You're not going to solve
this problem by reasoning with Iggy. Instead of talking, act!
Take charge! If you set the precedent of allowing him to control
this situation, then your troubles are just beginning. Take your
friend up on her kind offer. If she's willing to put up with Iggy's
screaming, take him out to her, hand him over, and walk away.

Just before the next time your friend comes, say this to
Iggy: "Guess what, Iggy? So-and-so is coming to take you to
school this morning. Remember how you screamed the last time
she came? Well, you can scream today, too! It's a fine day for
screaming."

When she pulls up, and he begins to scream, say, "Good for
you! That's a great scream! Let's go out to the car so everyone
else can hear you!"

I know, this sounds a bit crazy, but it works, believe me.
Several years ago, I gave the same advice to the mother of a
toddler who screamed every time she arrived at her morning
preschool program. The mother was convinced her child's reluctance to separate from her was indication of some deep-seated
insecurity (an example of the mischief "helping professionals"
have made in the world). I told her simply to encourage her
daughter to scream.

So the next time they were on their way to the program,
the mother began saying things like, "This is a fine morning for
screaming. You know, when you scream, I know you love me, so
please scream this morning, okay? And scream real, real loud,

because then I know you love me a lot!" When they arrived at the center, her daughter announced that she could walk in by herself. She probably didn't want to be seen with a mother who'd obviously gone over the edge. In any case, there was no more screaming.

A reader sent in what I thought was a great solution to getting a toddler to cooperate with being put in a car seat: She suggests parents purchase a second car seat in which to strap the child's favorite teddy bear. Strap "Teddy" in first, she says, then the child. Makes great sense!

Adventures On (and Around) the Great White Water Chair

It is not difficult to toilet train a child. Your great-grandmother could have told you that. Yet since her day, toilet training has become a highly stressful parenting task for the American mother, perhaps the most stressful of the preschool years. The difference, once again, is that your great-grandmother wasn't consuming professional parenting advice. In 1955, researchers from Harvard and Stanford universities determined that nearly 90 percent of American twenty-four-month-old children were accident-free. Today, it is the very rare child of that age who is out of diapers and using the potty consistently. That's because since the 1960s, pediatricians and child psychologists have been dispensing very bad toilet training advice. This very bad advice consists of five equally fallacious claims and recommendations:

1. Training a child before his or her second birthday requires force and is likely to result in psychological harm.
2. The older the child, the easier he or she will be to toilet train.
3. If left to their own devices, children will toilet train themselves with minimal parent support.
4. Parents should not attempt to train until the child displays a specific set of so-called readiness signs.
5. Once training begins, if the child has an accident, parents should put him back in diapers and try again later.

Taking these one at a time:

1. Your great-grandmother, who trained your grandparents before they were two, did not use force. She simply made her expectations perfectly clear. And there is no evidence that children who had been trained before their second birthdays suffer bruised psyches. This is pure, unadulterated, unscientific hogwash, and that's the mildest way I can put it.
2. As for it being easier to toilet train the older child, a question is in order: Is it easier to house train a four-month-old puppy or a one-year-old dog? Right! The dog owner who waits until his pet is a year old before starting to house train is going to pay the devil. The habit of releasing whenever and wherever the urge strikes is going to be hard for the older dog to overcome. And so it is with children. All historical evidence indicates that the season for toilet training is between eighteen and twenty-four months.
3. Saying that children will toilet-train themselves is akin to saying they will teach themselves to read and play the piano if left to their own devices. It's true that maybe one

in a thousand children *does* teach himself to read or play the piano, but that leaves 999 who need adult instruction. Some children will teach themselves to use the toilet. In the meantime, their parents will spend lots of unnecessary money on diapers and lots of unnecessary time changing them.

4. There are no readiness signs other than that the child can follow simple directions.

5. After training begins, if the child has an accident (which is inevitable), repeat your expectations and press on. Nothing could be more confusing to a child than parents who start, then stop at the first accident, then start again, then stop again, and so on. That's madness.

Let's go back to the dog comparison for a moment. In fact, there are several illustrative parallels between house training a dog and toilet training a child. First, neither the dog nor the child needs to be punished in order to learn bowel and bladder control. In both cases, punishment is a function of frustration on the part of the handler or parent, and in both cases, punishment will set the process back.

Second, in both cases, the keys to success are clear direction and encouragement. Shown the alternative, a puppy will quickly realize that eliminating outside the boundaries of one's living space is preferable to eliminating inside those boundaries (fouling one's own nest). Show the alternative, encourage the puppy's success, and the puppy will quickly realize the benefits of using the yard instead of the kitchen floor. Likewise, show an intelligent child the alternative to diapers, encourage the child's success, and the child will quickly realize the benefits to himself of using the toilet. And believe me when I say it must be clear to the child that the benefit of using the toilet accrues primarily to *him* before he will begin using the toilet voluntarily and successfully. He will not cooperate as readily if the parent is acting as if this business of toilet training is for *her* benefit, that it's something *she* wants for herself and *desperately* so.

The final parallels are perhaps the most important: In both house training a puppy and toilet training a child, one must (a) set the stage properly, (b) communicate expectations clearly, and (c) respond to mistakes appropriately. That's it! Does that sound complicated? No, of course it doesn't, and it isn't. It's simple, in fact, as you will shortly see.

The early (I use the term only relatively) approach to toilet training described herein has a number of advantages over readiness signs–based, later training:

- It respects a child's intelligence and abilities.
- Parents gain early independence along with the child—independence from diaper changing and the expense of disposables and their accessories (powder, anti-rash ointment, and so on).
- Training before age two respects and affirms the importance of parental authority and leadership.
- The child who experiences the benefits of early training is unlikely to develop the various problems associated with later training, including withholding, constipation (and resulting enlargement of the colon), and downright refusal to use the toilet.
- It is nonpsychological. Therefore, it liberates parents from the anxiety of thinking that one misstep in toilet training will scar the child's delicate psyche for life, thus enabling a calm, controlled approach to helping the child gain control.
- It is nonintellectual in that parents are not required to consult laundry lists of readiness signs or made to believe they have to understand the supposedly complex psychology of the child in order to properly and successfully train.
- Children trained before their second birthdays are happier kids because they have mastered bowel and bladder control early.
- Because training after the second birthday is much more likely to lead to power struggles than pre-two training,

parents who train early are going to have a happier parenting experience.

To further inspire you, listen to a mom who has used my approach, which I call "Naked and $75" (to be explained later) successfully with two children.

"I began Naked and $75 when my second child, a daughter, was eighteen months and one week old. Initially, the accidents well outnumbered the successes, but I pushed on and slowly but surely, things got better. It took about four weeks, but one day she just got it! She was nineteen months and five days old! That was ten days ago. This morning, we went shopping, and she had her first success on a public toilet! Needless to say, I'm thrilled! I didn't begin toilet training my first until she was twenty-seven months old. I also used Naked and $75 with her, and it was fairly easy, but this was even easier!"

Note that this mom had greater success when she started training earlier than she had with her first child—at eighteen months! And not only did Mom have greater success, but her child also had greater success. Cleanliness is a wonderful feeling.

The Preliminaries

As with many tasks, properly setting the stage is critical to the success of toilet training. This is not something to be initiated impulsively. Think it through in advance. Imagine the potential problems and visualize how you are going to deal with them. Don't be caught with your pants down, so to speak. The more prepared you are, the more smoothly this process will proceed.

Timing

Historical and cross-cultural data confirm beyond reasonable doubt that the peak season for toilet training is between eighteen and twenty-four months of age. This is not to say that children younger than eighteen months cannot be trained, because history tells us otherwise. Even today, a good number of parents testify to having successfully trained children as young as twelve months. There's no doubt about it, children younger than eighteen months are able to develop the requisite awareness, communication skills, and bladder and bowel control. Nonetheless, I'm generally in favor of holding off until eighteen months. I feel—and this is confirmed by many personal and professional experiences as well as considerable parent testimony—that the supervision and assistance needed to train a child younger than eighteen months involves a cost to the parent that outweighs the benefits. Whereas it may take four months to completely train a fifteen-month-old, that same child at eighteen months of age can probably be trained in four weeks—in both cases, training is completed at nineteen months.

The occasional parent reports that her child showed considerable interest in using the toilet well before eighteen months and that the child essentially trained herself with minimal parent support. That's a horse of a different color, the distinguishing variable being that the child initiated the learning process, not the parent. In the event your child initiates the toilet training process before she is eighteen months of age, by all means provide whatever support she needs to attain mastery, but restrain your enthusiasm lest you begin inadvertently hovering and micromanaging. Give your child the space she needs to feel that *she* is directing her learning, not you.

I have much stronger feelings about waiting past twenty-four months than I do about training before eighteen months. In the first place, children older than twenty-four months are more likely to have developed the knee-jerk defiance characteristic of the terrible twos. The eighteen-month-old Dr. Jekyll who delights in doing what his parents tell him to do is very likely to be a twenty-six-month-old Mr. Hyde who delights in doing the exact opposite of what his parents tell him to do. Add to this the fact that the habit of eliminating without consideration of time or place is much, much stronger in a twenty-six-month-old than in an eighteen-month-old.

Proper Preparation

As your child approaches eighteen months, decide when to best fit this important project into your schedule and lifestyle. In making this decision, keep in mind that you are going to have to make a full commitment for anywhere from two to six weeks, maybe longer. Keep in mind that children learn different things at different rates of speed. Even given equal IQs, some kids learn to read at age five, some at age six, but they're all likely to be reading at the same level by age nine. Getting upset at a child who's not learning to read "fast enough" isn't going to help. In fact, it will make matters much worse. So it is with toilet training.

Try not to overthink this, however. Too much thinking can result in a lot of self-doubt and anxiety. Prepare as well as you can. When you think you've covered all the bases, go!

A Potty or a Potty Seat?

Obviously, you'll need a child-size potty or padded potty seat. I recommend the former because potties (a) facilitate a toddler's need for self-sufficiency, (b) involve fewer safety concerns, (c) are portable, and (d) allow a parent to readily determine how much of which substance the child produced.

Show and Tell

After purchasing your potty or potties, you need to show your child how *you* (as well as other family members) use the toilet. For that, you need only leave the bathroom door open and invite him in with you to show him how things are done. Listen up, Dads! Until training is over and done with, and your child is no longer showing interest in what you're doing in the bathroom and how you do it, I highly recommend that you *sit down* to urinate. Have no fear, fellows, this is not going to compromise your masculinity. It's simply good common sense. You're going to want your child, whether male or female, to sit for both "Number One" and "Number Two." If boys (and even some girls) see their dads standing to pee, they're probably going to want to stand to pee, too, and I don't need to describe the likely result.

Parents ask, "Would it be helpful, John, to prepare my child by reading him a children's potty-training book or having him watch a children's potty-training video?"

No! Don't do that! Toilet training is no big deal, and anything you do that implies otherwise is going to increase the risk of resistance on the part of your child. So, no, I don't recommend children's potty-training books or videos. To be honest, I think these things are silly at best.

Designate a Primary Staging Area

When you begin, the potty or potties should be in plain view. The axiom "out of sight, out of mind" was never so apropos. If your child spends approximately equal time in two rooms—her bedroom and the den, for example—then put one potty in her bedroom and one in the den. If you live in a two-story house and your child spends significant time on the second level during the day, then I recommend one potty for each level. I recommend *against* putting the potty in the bathroom.

Some people bristle at that. They contend that a child should learn, from day one, that one goes to the bathroom in the bathroom, not in the living room or the den. These folks often reason thus: When a child makes the transition from a crib to a big bed, the bed stays in the bedroom, where the child sleeps. Similarly, when making the transition from diapers to a potty, the potty should be in the bathroom. That's a clever argument, but the two situations are not parallel. You don't have to *teach* a child how to go to sleep. You have to *teach* a child to use a potty. To help your child learn this new skill, it is best to have the potty where it will serve as a near-constant reminder of your new expectations. Having the potty within your usual daytime field of vision also means you're going to know when your child is using it, when she needs help, and when she needs additional guidance. But as I said, if this seems altogether too strange to you, put the potty in the bathroom.

As accidents decrease and successes increase, move each (or the) potty closer to the nearest bathroom. When two potties are in sight of one another, eliminate one of them. The primary potty might begin its life in the den, then move to the hallway that connects the den to the bathroom, then move down the hallway so it sits right outside the bathroom door, and then move into the bathroom itself.

Your Support Squad

Make sure you get your spouse, older siblings who are capable of lending helping hands, relatives who spend considerable time with your child, regular babysitters, and preschool or day care staff on board. Tell each person what you're doing and how they can be of help. If your child attends a day care program, the staff will probably be very cooperative. After all, having a toilet-trained child means one less child's diapers to change. Furthermore, toilet training tends to be contagious in toddler groups. One child using the potty elicits the interest of the other children, many of whom begin asking to use the potty, which is a day care center or preschool teacher's dream come true! While I generally recommend keeping your child at home as much as possible during the first week of training, a fully cooperative, enthusiastic day care or preschool teacher can be your best ally. If your child receives the same messages concerning the same expectation from other people with whom she spends significant time, it will definitely speed the process along.

Preparing YOU with Five C-Words

Arrange things so that you are able to remain at home as much as possible during the first week of training. Do that week's grocery shopping beforehand, along with other errands you can anticipate. If you work outside the home, take vacation or personal time. This all but ensures that you will be able to stay focused on the task at hand and provide a consistent learning environment for your child. However, do not go into this with the intent of being finished within a week because the likelihood is you won't be. A week of focused, albeit relaxed, training should get the project off the ground and to a point where your child is cruising fairly smoothly toward the finish line. Most important, you absolutely must approach toilet training with the understanding that once you get started, you are going to see it through until completion. An attitude of "We'll try this for a while and see if it works out" is almost surely going to doom the project to failure. In fact, your attitude is the most important variable of all. A proper attitude consists of the Five Cs: *cool, calm, collected, confident,* and *committed.*

- **Cool** means that you approach this as if it's the most natural thing in the world. Keep in mind that toilet training is no bigger a deal than teaching your child to feed himself with a spoon: You demonstrate, give whatever assistance is needed, and clean up the messes the child makes during the learning process. Let's further examine this comparison: You don't agonize over whether your child is ready to begin using a spoon. You accept that a certain amount of trial and error will be involved, and you resolve to be patient. You don't peruse the library for books on spoon training. You don't buy him a spoon that plays his favorite song when he manages to get it into his mouth without spilling its contents. You don't read your child picture books or show him videos of children using spoons. You don't jump up and down and clap and squeal the first time your child gets the spoon to his mouth successfully. You just say, "Good for you!" and let that be it. You don't reward him with stars or new toys for feeding himself. You let the mastery of the skill be its own reward. And so it should be with toilet training.

♦ **Calm** means that you communicate your expectations without fanfare or anxiety and respond to accidents without drama. And remember, you most surely are going to deal with accidents because every learning process is a matter of trial and *error*.

♦ **Collected** means your approach to the toilet training project is organized, not haphazard. Prepare yourself well, like a Boy Scout.

♦ **Confident** means you are absolutely certain of success and communicate that certainty to your child in a cool, calm, and collected manner.

♦ **Committed** means you are going to see this through to completion. You are not going to do what so many parents do: After starting toilet training, they experience more failure (accidents) than success, so they stop and put their child back in diapers. They wait a while, then try again, and so on. This "on again, off again" approach often results in a child of three or older who is still in diapers and who has become wary of and resistant to the idea of sitting on the toilet because toilet training has been, to this point, as much of a hassle for him as it has been for his mother.

It's going to make things much easier if you find a primary support person who will stand by your side for the duration of training. This person can be your mother, your best friend, your spouse, another mom who successfully toilet trained her child before or shortly after his or her second birthday, or your child's day care teacher—someone you can ask for advice, someone you can turn to if the going gets rough. Without such support, you are more likely to cave in at the first sign that things are not going exactly as planned.

Don't set a specific time frame as a goal, as in "My child will be toilet trained within two weeks." A goal of that sort will make you feel pressured and anxious, and you will communicate that pressure and anxiety to your child. The inevitable result: a child who balks at using the potty. Once you incorporate the Five Cs into your attitude, you have to go with the flow. (Am I clever with the puns or what?) If you set a specific date as a goal, you will most surely become a control freak where toilet training is concerned, unable to relax because you will be thinking constantly of a date that is looming ever closer.

The Whole Poop on "Naked and $75"

"Naked" means that during the actual training phase, your child is going to be naked or, if a boy, wearing only thin cotton underpants during the day. "$75" means that after your child has mastered using the toilet, you are going to call a carpet cleaner and pay approximately $75 to have him remove the stains and smell from your carpets. Naked and $75 consists of seven components and considerations:

1. **Set the stage properly.** Put your child's potty out in the open, in the area of the house where she spends most of her time during the day. Yes, even if that means the living room. Setting the stage properly also means getting rid of diapers, pull-ups, the changing table, and anything else that is associated with wearing diapers. All of this stuff should disappear. Keeping the accoutrements of a prior era around will only tempt you to turn back to them if the going gets

the least bit rough. If you give up smoking but keep a pack of cigarettes in the top drawer of your bedside table just in case, you will surely be back to smoking within a month. The same is true of keeping diapers on reserve when you are toilet training.

2. **Communicate your expectations clearly.** A parent's effectiveness as a disciplinarian depends more on how well the parent communicates expectations than on how well the parent manipulates reward and punishment (consequences). For most parents, toilet training is the first big disciplinary step they will take with their children. It is very important, therefore, that good disciplinary precedents be established during the toilet training process, and the most important of these precedents involves the proper use of speech that (a) is brief, straightforward, and devoid of persuasive explanations, (b) uses concrete rather than abstract terms, and (c) is directive. It is the difference between "It's time for you to use the potty now" and "It's been a long time since you last used the potty, so how about if we go sit and see if something comes out, and if it does, Mommy will give you a bowl of ice cream, okay?"

3. **Make it as simple as possible for your child.** This is where "naked" comes in. Let your child walk around the house naked or, in the case of a boy, wearing only the thinnest cotton underwear you can find. The idea is to have the "stuff" run down the child's legs. That's right! In order to replace the old habit—eliminating whenever and wherever she feels the urge—with the new habit of using the potty, the cues associated with the old habit must be eliminated as much as possible. One of those cues is bulky, absorbent material around the child's pelvic area. In other words, *to help your child learn something new, you need to get rid of the old.* Also, if you let your child walk around naked from the waist down,

she will immediately know when she has an accident, and so will you. When she feels the discomfort of stuff running down her legs, she will stand stock-still, look down, get a horrified look on her face, and begin to yell. Hearing her, you will arrive on the scene as soon as possible, probably while she's still in the act. If so, you should say with cool, calm, confidence, "Let's get you cleaned up, and then let's get the floor cleaned up. But first, listen to me. When you feel poo-poo or pee-pee about to happen, you need to go sit down on the potty, which is right over there," or something along those lines, something that is not scolding or critical but coolly and calmly directive.

4. **Respond properly to mistakes.** The first thing to keep in mind about mistakes, accidents, or whatever you call them, is they are inevitable. When they happen, respond matter-of-factly ("You had an accident, so let's get you cleaned up"), encouragingly ("I know you'll do better next time"), and instructively ("The next time you feel a poo-poo, go sit on your potty like Mommy showed you" or "Remember that pee and poop go in the potty"). Needless to say, yelling and other outbursts of frustration on your part are going to be counterproductive. If you discover an accident and don't know when it occurred, lead your child over to it and be very clear about your expectations, as in "Your pee/poop does not belong on the floor. It belongs in the potty. Go sit on the potty right now and see if you can poop or pee some more for Mommy." If you see telltale signs of needing to eliminate (the scrunched look, squeezing the legs together, pulling at or holding the genitals), don't ask, "Do you have to use the potty?" Remember the need for authoritative speech and say, "You need to use the potty. Go sit." (As opposed to something along the wimpy lines of, "Do you need to use the potty? Let's go sit on it and try to do something, okay?")

5. **Respond properly to successes.** Keeping your cool and remaining calm applies to toilet training successes as much as it does failures. Making a big deal of your child's successes is going to be as detrimental as overreacting to his failures. In both cases, the problem is calling too much attention to something that isn't a big deal. Making a big deal of success puts a child in the spotlight, and the minute a child is in the spotlight, resistance becomes more likely, no matter the issue. So, when your child has success, praise him, but make it *cool* praise, as in, "Hey! Good job! Isn't that fun? And isn't it nice that you don't have to wear diapers any more? Yep, it sure is!" For most kids, the simple act of carrying the potty to the bathroom, emptying it in the big potty, and flushing it down is going to be reinforcement enough. Don't do what one author of child care books advises: Reward your child's success with candy, gum, and shopping trips.

6. **Don't provide entertainment.** Don't entertain (read, sing, play games) or give food rewards to a child while he's on the potty. Approaches of that sort reflect parental anxiety and insecurity. For one thing, both entertainment and this kind of potty party require that the parent be present while the child is sitting. That's a recipe for increasing micromanagement. Furthermore, entertainment is likely to distract your child from the task at hand and result in a potty-sitting marathon that lasts fifteen to sixty minutes and ends without success.

7. **Keep your distance.** There is nothing that will more surely doom toilet training to frustration and failure than parental micromanagement, as in well-intentioned attempts to prevent the child from making mistakes. One of the reasons you are going to let your child walk around naked or almost naked is so you (hopefully) don't have to assist her in sitting on the potty, so that any involvement on your part can

be minimal. The less involved you are, the more effectively you let your child own the process. The parent who hovers anxiously over the child, constantly reminding the child to remember to sit on the potty, obsessively trying to get the child to sit for just a little while to see whether anything happens, and so on, is going to provoke resistance. Toddlers want to do *everything* themselves, so the trick here is to give them enough space, along with enough guidance, to make them think they're doing this completely on their own. If the child's resistance provokes parental frustration, maybe even outbursts of anger, the child will respond by becoming even more resistant, whether passively or actively.

Here's testimony from a mom who realized she was micromanaging. "When my first son was twenty-seven months, I began potty training with the 'Naked and $75' method. However, I couldn't relax about it. I was always hanging around him, trying to prevent accidents. For about six weeks he was successful some of the time but still had periodic accidents. Then I read one of your articles on the need to avoid micromanagement during training, and I was shocked. You were writing about me! I heeded your advice, and my son had very few accidents after that."

Okay, that's it. You now have your attitude straight and all the set pieces in place.

Let's Get Started!

You've made up your mind. You've decided whether to go with potty seats or potty chairs (or a combination), and you've decided where you're going to place them. For the last few weeks, you and your husband, and perhaps even older siblings, have let your child watch you go to the bathroom. The night before the not-so-big day, after your child went to sleep, you made everything associated with diapers disappear. You've read this book and wrapped yourself in the Five Cs: cool, calm, collected, confident, and committed. Nothing can stop you now!

Your child wakes up in the morning. You greet him, lift him out of his crib, lay him down, and remove his diaper. When you're done, you put only the thinnest (make sure they're really flimsy) cotton underwear on him. If your child is a girl, you leave her naked from the waist down. You take a deep breath and say, "You're not wearing diapers anymore. Today, Mommy and Daddy are going to teach you how to use the potty. Come with me, and I'll show you."

You put him down, take his hand, and take him to the nearest potty. You say, "This is your potty. It's just like Mommy and Daddy's, only smaller. You've seen Mommy and Daddy poop and pee on the potty, and now it's time for you to start pooping and peeing on your very own potty. I want you to sit on it and see how it feels. That's great! Most excellent! From now on, when you feel like you have to poop or pee, you just sit on this potty. If you need help, call Mommy or Daddy, and we'll help you. Okay, I'm going to go fix your breakfast now. While I'm fixing breakfast, see if you can poop or pee in your new potty."

And you're off and running!

A Word to the Wise About the Boy Problem

It goes without saying that the parents of a boy will need to teach him to push his penis down while on the potty so that his urine goes into the potty and not straight out over the top. Splashguards are meant to prevent this, but they are not always effective and sometimes wind up being a sitting hazard. If your son insists on standing like he's seen Daddy do, don't get in his way! If that's the case, you may want to locate the potty in the bathroom or a room that's not carpeted. Even so, put towels on the floor around the potty chair. This is obviously messier, but if your little fellow wants to do it standing up, it's worth letting him have his way as opposed to getting into a power struggle over sitting.

Stay the Course

If you initiate and your child resists, ask yourself whether you're anxious. Again, parental anxiety results in micromanagement (i.e., nervous questions like "Do you need to use the potty?" and "Let's go try to use the potty again, okay?"), and that is the number one cause of child resistance. If you're on pins and needles, it's time to remind yourself that teaching a child to use the toilet is no more worthy of anxiety than teaching a child to feed himself with a spoon.

Also, give it time. Rome wasn't built in a day, and a child is rarely trained in a week. After a few days, if your naked or barely covered child is still having more accidents than successes or just plain doesn't seem to be getting it, don't jump to the conclusion that he's not ready or some such foolishness. Stay the course. Some kids get it right away and some don't. Some take three days to train, and some are still pooping and peeing all over the place after a week. But if you stay the course for a week and are not seeing any progress, or your child takes one step forward and then one step back and then one step forward and so on, it's definitely time to up the ante, to apply some benign pressure to the process. That's where the potty bell and gate come into play.

The Potty Bell

A potty bell is nothing more than a small kitchen timer that emits an audible sound (preferably a buzzer or sustained tone) when a set time has expired, and it can help you organize your approach to toilet training, focus your child on the task at hand, reduce the likelihood of resistance, and help you avoid the inclination to micromanage. The concept is quite simple and practical: The timer signals to the child that it's time to sit on the potty. If you use an impersonal signal, any tendency on your child's part to resist will be effectively defused. *You* aren't telling your child to sit, the timer is.

Put the timer in the designated toilet training area, where your child can hear it when it rings or buzzes. Set it to go off after a certain amount of time has elapsed; I generally recommend an interval of sixty to ninety minutes, but as training unfolds, you can adjust the interval to more closely match your child's rhythms. You can also alter the interval to take special circumstances into consideration. For example, if your child usually has a bowel movement twenty to thirty minutes after he eats lunch, then set the first after-lunch interval at twenty minutes. To increase the likelihood that your child will experience success when he sits on the potty, I recommend that you have him drink more water than usual.

Introduce your child to the potty bell by telling him something along these lines: "This is a potty bell. It tells children when to sit on the potty. When it rings, that means you need to go sit on the potty until you poop or pee. I'm going to put the potty bell right here so you can hear it."

A simple explanation is best. Set the timer for the interval you've decided upon. When it rings, direct your child to sit on the potty in a casual yet commanding fashion: "There's the potty bell! That means you need to go sit on the potty."

Because your child is naked, or almost so, he shouldn't need any help from you. When he's seated himself successfully, your job is to go find something, anything, to do so you don't hover anxiously over him, waiting for him to produce something. As you walk away, say something like, "Let me know when you've pooped or peed so I can help you put it in the big potty." By walking away and giving your child the space he needs to feel independent, you not only communicate your confidence to him but also activate a very important toilet-training axiom: The more successful you are at letting go of the urge to hover, the more likely it is your child will be able to successfully let go.

Initially, you'll have to prompt your child to remember what to do when the potty bell rings, and some children may need a more authoritative prompt or more help than others. But if you let your child own the learning that's taking place, it should not take more than a few days before prompts will be completely unnecessary; your child will hear the bell and immediately go sit on the potty.

The two primary advantages to using the potty bell are these:

- Because the signal to go sit on the potty is coming from an impersonal source as opposed to you, any tendency your child may have to resist is minimized, if not completely neutralized.
- Any tendency on your part to vigilantly hover and anxiously ask, every few minutes, "Do you have to sit on the potty?" is likewise minimized, if not completely eliminated.

Thus, toilet training's two biggest stumbling blocks—resistance from the child and micromanagement on the part of the parent—are effectively removed, clearing the way for your child to feel he is in control of the process and his successes are his and his alone. Mastery is made of those feelings. Within a short time that may vary from a few days to a few weeks, your child will figure out that certain internal sensations mean he needs to eliminate, and he will begin sitting on the potty and producing without a prompt from the potty bell. At that point, the training is off the ground, and you can put the potty bell away for your next child.

The Gate

A childproof safety gate is a handy way of partitioning off the designated toilet training area and keeping your child within it. Restricting the child's field of freedom during training makes sure he doesn't lose sight of the new expectation. It also makes the job of supervision a lot easier for you.

A gate can also come in handy in the event your child is resistant toward the notion of sitting on the potty or seems completely uninterested. Neither resistance nor lack of interest is an indication your child isn't ready. Some children may balk at the notion of sitting on the potty simply because it's something new. Others may balk simply because on the day their parents begin their training, they woke up on the wrong side of the bed, disinclined to cooperate with anything their parents ask of them. At the other end of the reaction spectrum are the occasional kids who, when introduced to the potty, act like it's not there. It's the rare child who doesn't seem to mind having stuff run down his or her legs, but it happens. In any case, a gate is the solution. It can be used in one of two ways:

- **To cordon off a certain area.** For example, if you've decided to put the potty in the doorway between his playroom and the family room because that's where your toddler spends most of his or her time during the day, then use a gate or gates to section off that area.
- **To confine your child to the bathroom.** If—being the strong-willed parent you are—you decide to defy my authority and put the potty in the bathroom, using the

potty bell becomes all but essential. You may also find that because the bathroom is unquestionably the most boring place in the house besides the coat closet, your child won't stay in the bathroom long enough to produce anything. To prevent a power struggle from developing, with you trying to keep your child in the single most boring place in the house and your child trying his best to escape, use the gate. When the potty bell rings, direct him to the bathroom and close the gate. Tell him to call when he has something to show you and walk away. Under the circumstances, it is not important that he sit on the potty while he's in the bathroom; it's only important that he stay in there, with his potty, until he feels the urge. Then he can sit and release and call you and show you and get out of there. Freedom is great reinforcement for proper behavior, so this probably won't take long.

Continue using the gate until your child is going to the bathroom independently when the potty bell rings, and continue using the bell until your child is going to the bathroom without that cue. If you use the gate for a couple of weeks, things seem to be going reasonably well, and you want to see what happens without the gate, fine. But do not hesitate to bring back the gate at the first sign of resistance or uninterest. The occasional child even likes the gate because of the structure (and therefore security) it provides. For example, one little girl of twenty-one months who hated the gate at first ended up asking her mother for it! Just the same, your child will let you know, one way or another, when he doesn't need the gate anymore.

The Transition to a Potty Seat

When training is pretty much over and done, you can then transition to a toilet seat. But again, set things up so that your child needs a minimum of help from you. Where there is a toilet seat, there should be a stool so he can get up on the toilet himself. And when you get to that stage, he'll no longer be naked; he'll be wearing clothing. Make sure it's loose fitting with an elastic waist so he can pull down his own pants with ease.

When You Leave the House

Until your child has transitioned to a potty seat at home, you really cannot expect him to use a public toilet, and *you most definitely do not want to put him back in diapers or pull-ups when you leave your house.* So until that transition has been made, I recommend you take his potty with you and be proactive about its use. Don't wait until your child signals the need to go and then dash madly to your car. Instead, when you arrive at your destination, say, "Before we go into the store, you need to sit on the potty." Don't ask, "Do you need to use the potty before we go into the store?" The latter, being a question, is not authoritative. It is equivocal and is likely to evoke a "No!" Remember that you're going to be dealing with a toddler, and toddlers, even some who are younger than two, take every opportunity to use their favorite word.

If your toddler sits on the car potty for a few minutes and nothing happens, then go into the store, first reminding him, "Tell me if you feel a [whatever you call it]." Fifteen to thirty minutes into the shopping trip, say, "It's time to try and use the potty again," and head for the car. Again, don't say, "Do you feel anything?" or "Are you ready to try using the potty again?" or "It's time to use the potty again, okay?" Declare the intent, proceed to your car, put your child on the potty, and stand aside. Read something. Sing a song to yourself while contemplating the clouds (I recommend songs with images of water, like "Raindrops Keep Fallin' on My Head" or "Up a Lazy River"). In any case, don't stand there anxiously like you're waiting to find out if you won the lottery. You may have to take your child to the car several times before something happens. A tip: During times like this, it helps to have your child drink lots of water. Water, mind you, not soda or anything sugar-sweetened. Drinks of that sort don't run through as quickly. They're bad for your child anyway.

Questions?

Q *I now realize that we waited entirely too long to begin training. Our daughter is almost three. Although we're fairly convinced she knows how to use the toilet (and has, on occasion, for other people), she's all but oblivious to it when we're around. Is there anything we can do to turn back the clock?*

A Indeed, it's possible to jump-start a child's interest in and willingness to use the toilet. All you need to do is provide the structure and stimulation to get the skill to emerge.

Tell your daughter that you went to the doctor and he told you it's time for her to begin using the potty. Tell her the doctor gave you a potty bell. Say, "The doctor says this potty bell will help you learn to use the potty. When you hear it ring, that means it's time for you to go sit on the potty."

Set the potty bell to ring five or ten minutes after she wakes up in the morning and from her naps. Otherwise, set it to ring every ninety minutes to two hours, depending on what you guess-timate to be her schedule.

Invoking the authority of the doctor is a creative way of preventing resistance to certain expectations you are trying to convey. I recommend using doctors over other authority figures (ministers, the police, television newscasters, the president); doctors are regarded as so much larger than life in our culture that by the time a child is two-and-a-half, her perceptions of doctors have already been enlarged. So if you want your two-year-old to go to bed at a certain time, try, "The doctor says this is when you should go to bed." Or if you want your toddler to sit cooperatively in her car seat, "The doctor says that when you ride in the car, you have to sit in this seat."

Properly but conservatively invoked, the doctor becomes a benign means of bypassing power struggles.

Q *I've been trying to toilet train my twenty-six-month-old son for several months now. He will have a good day, then a few bad days, then a good day, and so on. Sometimes he cooperates, and sometimes he won't. I'm getting tired of changing pull-ups. Also, he seems to be getting more stubborn with each passing day. For example, when we leave the house, he wants to wear his Barney pajamas. I have to physically overpower him to get "outside" clothes on him. What should I do? Could it be that he's simply not ready?*

A Well, you unwittingly told me how you can solve this problem, but first let me make it clear that this is not a problem of readiness. A human being is ready to be toilet trained sometime between eighteen and twenty-four months. That age child can understand the expectation, attune to the physical signals, and manage the procedure.

The fact that your son has occasional good days tells me he knows what to do. Your use of the phrase "sometimes he will cooperate, sometimes he won't" tells me you are micromanaging. You're hovering, enticing, and otherwise trying to force the issue, trying to get him to cooperate. You're making a big deal of this, and the bigger you make the deal, the more uncooperative he becomes.

You've also made the common mistake of using pull-ups during training. Pull-ups feel very much like diapers, which the child associates with permission to release at will. Learning to control what you have not controlled for two years requires a different set of cues. Let him wear his Barney pajamas, and only his Barney pajamas, with nothing on underneath, everywhere—inside, outside, to the shopping center, the opera. Everywhere he goes, Barney goes. Believe me, no one will be scandalized by the sight of a toddler in public wearing Barney pajamas, and you won't be reported to the fashion police.

Put the potty out in the open, where he spends most of his time during the day. If that's the living room, so be it. If the potty is out of sight, it's also out of mind. Tell him he can wear his Barney pajamas as long as he doesn't wet them or poop in them. If he wets or poops on Barney, he has to take Barney off so Barney can take a bath, and he can't wear Barney again until Barney is dry. Meanwhile, he has to wear thin cotton underpants. If you want to turn this up a notch, tell him that he can't put Barney back on, even when Barney is dry, until he uses to potty successfully.

This is nothing more than a variation on Grandma's Rule: When you do what I, the parent, want you to do, you can do what you want to do. You want him to use the potty. He wants a close personal relationship with Barney. Ta-da! When he wakes up in the morning, you have to take his Barney pajamas off in order to take off his diaper. Okay then. Simply tell him he has to use the potty before Barney can go back on.

From that point, use a kitchen timer as a potty bell. Set the timer to go off once every hour or on whatever timetable seems to suit your son's need-to-go schedule. Don't lead him to the potty, stand over him while he goes, and so on. Just let the timer be the reminder and stay out of it. Praise his successes, of course, and make no big fuss about his mistakes. I'll wager that not getting to wear Barney will be enough to seal the deal.

Q *Our twenty-seven-month-old daughter has just begun to use the toilet on her own. She is very proud of herself, as are we, but we want to be careful not to push. How much should we remind her of the potty? Should we still put diapers on her at night, during long rides in the car, and when we're going shopping, or will this confuse her?*

A As your daughter learns to use the toilet, she is also learning an important thing about independence and responsibility: They both feel good. Therefore, the less involved you are, the better. Remember that she is doing this for herself, and let her success belong to her. You don't even need to praise her a lot, because the reward comes from acquiring the skill. In fact, if you heap praise on her, she may stop using the toilet altogether. How else would she be able to get you to back off?

Reinforce the pride she takes in herself. Take her to the store and let her help you pick out some big-girl panties. When she's obviously looking for some praise from you, give her a hug and a kiss, but don't act like a cheerleader. Likewise, treat her inevitable accidents matter-of-factly and with words of understanding and encouragement. Let her tell you how involved she wants you to get. She will almost certainly need some help from you in learning to clean herself properly. Beyond that, you can tell her to call you if she needs you.

Continue using diapers at night for a while, but try a few nights without them every few weeks to see if she remains dry. Night dryness usually follows successful daytime toilet learning by three to six months. Don't give any reminders at all unless some major interruption of her routine is about to take place. These would include long car rides and trips to shopping centers. During car rides, stop every couple of hours and say, "It's time for all of us to use the potty." In shopping centers, show her that the stores have bathrooms and say, "Be sure to let us know if you need to use one."

Above all else, remember the musical maxim: She's gotta do it *her way.*

Q *Our almost-three-year-old daughter learned to use the toilet, and pretty much on her own, shortly after her second birthday. After nearly a year, however, she is still not consistently dry at night. She might go two or three nights without an accident, then wet every night for two weeks. As a result, we continue to put her diaper on at bedtime. Is there some way of helping her learn to stay dry at night?*

A I'd suggest you put your daughter to bed without diapers. During her first two years of life, the feel of wearing a diaper became associated with permission simply to release when her bladder became full. Wearing a diaper to bed, therefore, makes it all but inevitable that she'll wet in it.

Furthermore, the mere fact that you put a diaper on her at bedtime tells her you don't expect her to be dry through the night. Children tend to behave in accordance with the expectations their parents convey, however unspoken those expectations may be. In a sense, by continuing to put diapers on her at night, you're giving her tacit permission to wet in them.

For the time being, and until she is consistently dry through the night, I'd recommend that you put her to bed in a loose-fitting nightie with nothing on underneath. This will increase the likelihood that she will be sensitive to the pressure of a full bladder while she's sleeping and hold off going until she wakes up. And one more thing: Use a waterproof mattress cover for the duration.

Q *Our three-year-old daughter was successfully toilet trained at two. About a month ago, she began having bowel movements in her pants. At first, we thought she might have a physical problem, but her doctor says she's perfectly healthy. At his advice, we started making her sit on the toilet for thirty minutes after every meal and whenever she looked like she needed to go, but that didn't work. Now, when she has an accident, which is nearly every day, we clean her up, spank her, and put her in her room for a while. This isn't working either. What will?*

A A regression in toileting skills such as you describe is usually triggered by a major change in the child's life: a move, parents separating, the birth of a sibling, or the start of day care. In some cases, however, the problem begins spontaneously, without apparent cause. Whatever the reason—or lack of one—it's important to realize that your daughter is not doing this manipulatively to get attention or engage you in a power struggle. Young children don't think like that. They *respond* to attention, and they fall into certain behavior patterns as a result of attention, but they don't consciously think in terms of getting it. In all likelihood, she had an accident, you made a big deal over it, and she had another one. The more of a big deal you made of her accidents, the more of a big deal they became.

I can understand your frustration, but frustration only brings out the worst in parents. It muddles their thinking and causes them to do things that make problems worse instead of better. Punishing your daughter will do just that, as you've already discovered. Instead, give her responsibility for the problem.

First, review things with her: "When you were a baby, you wore diapers and pooped in them. Then you learned to use the potty and started wearing big-girl panties. Now you've started pooping in your pants again, like when you were a baby. You've forgotten how to use the potty, so Mommy and Daddy are going to help you remember. When you poop in your panties, we're going to take you to the bathroom and leave you there to clean yourself up and rinse out your panties. Being in the bathroom and cleaning yourself will help you remember to use the potty next time."

Then teach her how to swish her soiled panties around in the toilet until they're fairly clean and hang them up to dry. Teach her how to clean herself as well. (You may also want to keep a supply of clean underpants in the bathroom for her.) These are things three-year-olds can be taught to do. It isn't important that she do a perfect job, however. What's important is that she take on the biggest share of responsibility for the problem. From this point on, when an accident occurs, respond calmly: "Uh-oh, you forgot again. You need to go to the bathroom and wash out your panties and clean yourself like I taught you."

In anywhere from a few days to a few weeks, your patience and the fact that you've put the problem gently on her shoulders will begin to pay off.

No More Bedtime Blues

Where bedtime is concerned, sleep isn't the primary issue. Oh, sure, you want your child to go to bed and go to sleep. You want the day to be over and done with. But bedtime's bigger picture is all about parent and child learning to separate from one another. How a parent responds to a young child's resistance to being put to bed and left alone to fall asleep will have long-standing influence on how the child processes and reacts to other separation events (e.g., being left with sitters, going to day care for the first time, going to school).

If a mother interprets her eighteen-month-old son's protests at bedtime as evidence that she's not responding adequately to his needs (whatever she thinks they are), and she reacts by lying with him or rocking him until he's asleep, he's all but certain to object every time she tries to separate from him, no matter the circumstances. The end result: a mother who feels increasingly guilty and inadequate and a child who is snagged on the issue of separation.

On the other hand, if this same mother accepts her son's protests as the price they both must pay to clear this hurdle, and she continues to communicate firmly but gently that he must go to bed at a certain time and fall asleep on his own, the hurdle will eventually be cleared, to the lasting benefit of all concerned.

I learned how to put children to sleep the hard way. Our first child, Eric, didn't sleep through the night until he was two and one-half. Colic was a contributing factor, but the real problem was his parents. Early on, we got into the habit of rocking him to sleep. And so he got into the habit of needing to be rocked to sleep. Since he didn't learn to fall asleep on his own, he woke up several times throughout the night, whereupon one of us would rock him back to sleep.

Finally, shortly before Willie became pregnant with our second child, Eric began sleeping through the night. I'm sure it was divine intervention. In any case, we determined we would not repeat the same mistake. From day one, we put Amy down early in the evening and let her cry herself to sleep. I developed the method of going in every five or ten minutes, reassuring her that everything was still okay, and then leaving again. During these interventions, which never lasted more than a minute, we never picked her up. The goal wasn't to get her to stop crying, but to simply let her know that we were still there, watching over her. Within a couple of months, Amy was sleeping through the night. But that wasn't the end of the story.

Bedlam at Bedtime

Midway through her third year, Amy began turning bedtime into a game of "Let's See Just How Crazy You Can Make Your Parents." Five minutes after we had tucked her in bed, she'd be downstairs, asking, "When's my birthday?" or "What're you talking about?" or "Who was in the truck that jus' went by the house?" One of us would answer her question, lead her back to bed, tuck her in, go downstairs, and wait. Sure enough, five minutes or so later she'd be standing in front of us, looking as innocent as a kitten.

"What is it, Amy?"

"Ummmm, I forgot to tell you somethin'."

"What did you forget to tell us, Amy?"

"Ummmm, I, ummmm, watched *Mister Rogers* today."

And back to bed she'd go (not of her own free will), until she thought of something else to ask or tell, or a reason to be scared and call for us, or a request, as in, "I need orange juice."

By ten o'clock, our patience having run out, one of us—usually me—would experience cerebral meltdown. I'd start babbling incoherently and, eyes glowing red, would chase Amy back upstairs, beating my chest like something out of *Where the Wild Things Are*. This would terrify Amy so much she'd be up another two hours, crying. It was usually midnight before the house was quiet.

After several months of this, realizing that persuasion, threat, and fear were not going to work, we thought of a way to outsmart her (no small feat, since children this age are much, much smarter than their parents). One night when I was tucking Amy in, I leaned over and whispered, "When we leave your room, Amos, you can fool us by quietly closing your door, turning on the light, and playing with your toys. If you're very, very quiet, we won't hear you! Mommy and Daddy will think you're asleep, and we won't get mad, and you can play until you fall asleep. Doesn't that sound like fun? Yes, it does!" Her eyes got big, and she giggled.

"But if you make a noise, or open your door," I went on to say, "then we'll have to put you back to bed and turn out your light. So let's see if you can fool us tonight, Amos. Let's see how quiet you can be."

Magic! From that night forward, Amy delighted in fooling us. Every evening, as we tucked her in, we'd remind her of our gullibility. We'd share a conspiratorial giggle with her, go downstairs, and revel in freedom from parenthood. A child's bedtime is, after all, for the sake of the child's parents.

The Family Bed . . . Not!

Whenever I write on the subject of bedtime in my syndicated newspaper column, I receive complaints from folks who believe in what is called the family bed, from a book of the same title by Tine Thevenin, guru of the family sleeping movement. Thevenin, a Minnesota homemaker, solved bedtime problems with her two children by bringing them into the marital bed. The family bed banner has been taken up by the La Leche League and pediatrician Dr. William Sears, author of several books on what's known as attachment parenting.

Family bed advocates claim that children are traumatized psychologically by the act of being abandoned by their parents at bedtime. This trauma supposedly leads to all manner of emotional problems. In short, the purveyors of this psychobabble go to absurdly melodramatic lengths to lay a guilt trip on parents who choose not to play musical beds every evening. For instance, here are the opening paragraphs of a *Parents Magazine* article extolling the virtues of family bundling:

> *For thousands of American kids, every night is the loneliest night of the week come 9:00 p.m., when their happy, loving families turn abruptly into untouchables. Junior is sent to his lonely bed, freshly made up with Donald Duck sheets. After a brief kiss and a warning look . . . his parents avert their eyes, for there are few sights sadder than the thin back of a child as he goes off to face the night alone. His tiny wing bones quiver with betrayal, and there is that awful moment at the foot of the stairs when he turns to fix Mommy and Daddy with one last imploring look.*

From that tear-jerk beginning, the author drew on Thevenin and others to debunk some of the supposed myths that lurk behind the oh-so-absolutely dreadful and destructive practice of putting children to sleep in their own beds, including the myth that sleeping alone promotes independence.

Trouble is, that's not a myth.

The point of assigning a specific bedtime for children and putting them down in their own beds, in their own rooms, is twofold: First, it gives parents much-needed time for themselves and each other. Second, bedtime is an exercise in separation and independence (also known as autonomy, self-reliance, and self-confidence). It is, in fact, the first of many such exercises to come. The manner in which parents handle it sets an important and enduring precedent.

Separation always involves a certain amount of anxiety. It is often frightening for a child and, assuming his parents are sensitive and caring people, it will be discomforting for them as well. The problem of separation, of moving from dependency toward a state of confident self-reliance is what growing up is all about. During the day, it's called standing on one's own two feet. At night, it's called sleeping in one's own bed.

In his best-selling book *The Road Less Traveled,* psychiatrist Scott Peck says that many people never learn to accept the inherent pain of living. When confronted with a problem, they either attempt an impatient, knee-jerk solution or try to ignore it altogether. Parents who spank their children because they cry at bedtime fall into the first category. Parents who let their children sleep with them fall into the second.

In Peck's terms, parents and children sleeping together is a way of avoiding a problem in the hopes that someday, somehow, it will miraculously resolve itself. Unfortunately, life will probably deal a different hand to family bed practitioners. The child whose parents avoid facing the pain of separation never receives complete, implicit permission to separate from them. As the years go by, his parents' continuing failure to confront and resolve this fundamental issue can grow into a huge obstacle to healthy growth and development.

In addition, if parents sleep together and separate from the child, that enhances the child's view of the marriage not only as a separate entity within the family but also as the most important relationship in the family. A child who sleeps with his or her parents is in danger of not achieving that understanding, of feeling wrongly that the marriage is a threesome. Coming to grips with the fact that the husband–wife relationship is paramount in the family helps the young child divest of self-centeredness, acquire a sense of independence, and move securely toward eventual emancipation. A child cannot achieve autonomy unless parents first establish the autonomy of their marriage. Although it may look like a very nurturing arrangement, the family bed actually extends dependency and interferes significantly with emotional growth.

At some point, nearly all young children cry at bedtime. Naturally, their cries make us want to draw them protectively closer. But protection of this nature is not always in a child's best interests. It is essential to the success of the emancipation process that children learn to deal with separation. Parents must show the way, and bedtime is one of the most opportune moments to begin the lessons. It's a big deal, to be sure, but as big deals go, not really that difficult at all.

Numerous parents who identify themselves as practitioners of attachment parenting have pointed out to me that children in primitive cultures always sleep with their parents. That's true, but these folks make the mistake of comparing apples to watermelons. In other cultures and other times, children have slept with their parents only when there were no other options. For instance, it would have been impractical, perhaps even deadly, for our prehistoric ancestors to hold out for a three-bedroom cave. Nor does it make sense for nomadic peoples to lug three-bedroom tents from site to site or for Eskimos to waste valuable time and energy building three-bedroom igloos.

It's also true that as soon as primitive cultures emerge from the Stone Age and begin building dwellings that consist of more than one room, children and parents begin sleeping in separate beds, usually in separate rooms. Furthermore, the notion that civilized cultures should emulate primitive ones is rather absurd. Should we also hang shrunken heads around our homes to ward off evil spirits? Finally, children in primitive cultures never leave the villages they grow up in. That may be the reason why those villages remain primitive. The fact that a certain child-rearing practice is or was common to more primitive cultures may qualify it as more natural, but we should not confuse natural with most desirable or healthy. If the reader is interested in pursuing these issues further, I've written an entire chapter on the farce of attachment parenting in *Parent-Babble* (Andrews McMeel, 2012).

In the following section, I respond to questions about bedtime that are typically asked by parents of toddlers. Because no one solution works for all children—even those of similar developmental status—I've made it a point to describe different solutions to problems that may appear similar, if not identical. It's up to the reader to choose the solution that best fits the particulars of the situation and the personalities of the adults and child involved.

Questions?

Q *Do you feel the same way about letting a young child crawl into his or her parents' bed in the morning?*

A Ah, yes, all rules have their exceptions, and this one, too, can be suspended under certain special circumstances. These include when the child is ill, or is recovering from an experience that has temporarily upset his or her security (the death of a pet, for instance), or for a night or two after the family has moved to a new home, thus giving the child time to adjust to the new surroundings.

I have no problem, either, with letting a child crawl into bed with parents in the morning for some cuddle time. I see absolutely no parallel between these temporary or short-term exceptions and letting children share the marital bed on a nightly basis, all night long.

Q *Our eighteen-month-old daughter won't go peacefully to sleep at night. As soon as she hits the mattress, she begins to wail. We've tried keeping her up until she's absolutely exhausted, but the wailing still results. Please don't tell us to let her cry it out because we just can't. Besides, she's already proven she can scream nonstop for almost an hour. The only thing that seems to work is rocking her to sleep, which takes about twenty minutes, then staying in there and rubbing her back for another ten or fifteen minutes once we put her in the crib. The added problem is, if she goes down crying, she almost always wakes up screaming in the middle of the night. There must be a better way!*

A Indeed, there is a better way to put an infant to sleep. Known as "Rosemond's Guaranteed No-Mo Sleepless Nights," it consists of three easy steps to permanent nighttime bliss, and at the same time it answers the question, "How do you keep 'em down in the bed after they've seen the alternative?" Here's the solution:

◆ Set a definite bedtime and stick to it. Do not, I repeat, do not try to wear an infant down by keeping her up long after reasonable people have gone to bed. Contrary to popular belief, the later you keep an infant up, the more agitated she will become and the more difficult bedtime will be when it finally arrives. Instead of waiting for a signal from your daughter that she's ready for sleep, make the decision for her. Somewhere between seven-thirty and eight-thirty in the evening is probably reasonable.

◆ Thirty minutes before bed, start putting her through a set bedtime routine—a bath, a snack, and a story. When the appointed hour arrives, put her down with a brief tucking-in ceremony and promptly leave the room, screams notwith-standing.

◆ Assuming she does scream, go back to her room every five minutes and repeat the tucking-in ceremony. If you must, lay her back down, reassure her that the world as she knows it still exists, that you are still a part of her life, kiss her, and exit stage left. Do not pick her up, and do not stay longer than one minute. Five minutes later, if she's still at it, go back in and repeat the procedure. Five minutes later, if she's still at it, repeat the procedure. Get my drift? (I'm going to stop here and mention that I've been accused of pirating this method from a well-known book on children's sleep-ing problems. *Au contraire.* I can assure the reader that I described this method in my newspaper column several years before that book was published.)

◆ Sooner or later, your daughter will begin to tire of this foolishness, and her screams will turn to whimpers. At this point, you should extend the interval to ten minutes, or whatever your common sense and intuition advise. If she shifts back into full throttle, return to the five-minute plan. True, she may scream for a couple of hours at first, but after several nights of this, she will scream less and less with every passing night. After a few weeks, she will scream at bed-time for only a few minutes, if at all. Look at it this way: At present, you spend anywhere from forty-five minutes to an hour getting her to sleep, more if you count the fact that you are keeping her up much too late to begin with. With the method just described, if she screams for two hours, you will have gone back into her room no more than twenty-four times, for less than a minute each time. This means you will spend only twenty minutes or so putting her to sleep—an immediate 50 percent reduction in time spent!

- ◆ If she wakes up in the middle of the night, repeat the five-minute plan until she falls back to sleep. Because she is likely to wake up in the middle of the night for at least the first few nights, I'd recommend that you initiate the plan on a Friday or some other night when you don't have to go to work the next morning.

I have yet to hear that this plan has failed (when parents hang in there, that is). Just call me "The Sandman."

Q *When we put our eighteen-month-old daughter to bed, she gets on her hands and knees and rocks back and forth, gently banging her head into the headboard. If one of us stays with her and sings her a song while rubbing her back, she doesn't do it. If we leave her room before she is asleep, however, she'll cry for a minute or two and then start rocking and head banging. This has become distressing to us. We worry that the repeated banging could cause damage. Furthermore, we don't understand why she would deliberately hurt herself.*

A You're making this much too complicated. Lots of infants and toddlers put themselves to sleep by getting on their hands and knees and rocking back and forth. In the process, some accidentally discover the pleasures of head banging.

In some mysterious way, the combination of the rocking motion and the gentle cranial stimulation helps these kids fall asleep. In this sense, it's what's known as a *transitional activity*, one that actually assists the child in moving from being awake to being asleep. Children who invent activities such as these for themselves may have a generally easier time making transitions than children who are less resourceful.

Why rocking and head banging? Who knows? It's easy to understand how the rocking motion would be soothing, but the head banging is a bit more difficult to explain. Have these kids discovered a relatively harmless way of slowly knocking themselves unconscious? All kidding aside, it's nothing to fret over. You haven't done anything wrong, and contrary to your fears, your daughter isn't going to inflict brain damage on herself. It's not a nervous habit, nor is it a symptom of insecurity. And it's much better for all concerned that she put herself to sleep in this manner than to become dependent on being rocked to sleep by one of you at bedtime.

I'm fairly certain that bedtime head-bangers experience no pain whatsoever. Remember that a young child's skull is fairly elastic, more like cartilage than bone. It absorbs impact much more efficiently than our hard heads. What looks painful to us is probably quite pleasurable. I've never heard of bedtime head-bangers looking punch-drunk in the morning.

Q *Our twenty-two-month-old son has recently developed a sleeping problem. He's always been easy to put to bed and began sleeping through the night at an early age. Lately, however, he has been waking up two or three times a night. He gets out of bed, stands in the doorway, and whimpers until one of us gets up and puts him back in bed. He doesn't fight us. In fact, he falls back to sleep quickly and quietly. Getting up several times a night is becoming a real hassle, but if we ignore him, he just gets louder and louder until we give in. What could be causing this problem, and what should we do about it?*

A This is the result of two influences. The first occurs sometime toward the end of the second year of life, when most children cycle through a phase of separation anxiety that usually lasts about three months. During this time, the growth of independence seems to stall and the child's requests for reassurance and closeness increase. Parents of children this age often describe them as being more clingy and whiny. This brief developmental glitch remains a mystery, but studies have shown children will get over it more quickly if their parents simply give them the reassurance they're asking for. The second influence has to do with neurological developments that are occurring around this time, developments that cause changes in a child's sleep patterns. As a result, it's not unusual for a toddler who has been sleeping through the night suddenly to begin waking up one or more times a night. As neurological development stabilizes, the child's sleep pattern will follow suit.

So regard your son's sleeping problem as something like a growing pain—just one of those things that happen in the course of normal growth and development. Like all other such things, if you handle it properly, it will pass in due time, leaving not a trace of ever having terrorized your nights.

It seems that your son is no more used to waking up in the middle of the night than you are, and he is just as upset about it. After all, the world is a quite different and frightening place when all the lights are out. So he sticks close to the security of his room and cries out for some reassurance. You should count your lucky stars. He could be wanting to get in bed with you or you to get in bed with him. He could be fighting going back to bed or screaming his lungs out for an hour or so. Or all of the above. As it is, he's asking for two minutes of your time, two or three times a night. That's a total of six minutes—a small and temporary price to pay.

If you will simply go to him quickly and calmly, and gently put him back to bed with a few reassuring words, he'll get over this in a few months, max. On the other hand, if you continue dealing with his night waking as if it were a behavior problem (e.g., ignoring him, becoming angry with him), it will almost certainly develop into one. The choice is yours.

Q *Our son turned two several months ago. We probably should have given him a separate bedroom long ago, but it's been more convenient to have him in with us (the second bedroom is upstairs). He goes to bed easily in his crib around nine o'clock and usually sleeps the night. Occasionally, however, he will wake up and want to get in bed with us. To further complicate matters, he's almost climbing out of his crib. First, how and when should we move him from our room to the second bedroom? Second, how and when should we make the change from crib to regular bed?*

A Your son is certainly old enough to make both transitions, but I'd take them one at a time, starting with the move to a regular bed. There's no mystery to accomplishing this. When he's still in your quarters, dismantle his crib and put a single-bed mattress on the floor. Let him sleep there until he gets the feel of it and is no longer rolling out. This should take a month or so. When he's over this first hurdle, put the mattress in its frame and let him get used to that.

For safety's sake, given the fact that the second bedroom is upstairs, wait to move him out of your room until he is no longer waking up in the middle of the night. Even then, put a childproof gate at the top of the stairs. Better safe than sorry. When you feel comfortable with the whole idea, prepare his room, involving him as much as possible. When things are ready, move his bed (and him) in there with much hoopla. There. The job is done.

Q *Our thirty-month-old daughter won't let us out of her bedroom at night. We begin getting her ready for bed around seven-thirty.*

After her bath, a snack, and a story, we'd like to turn out her light and leave. No such luck. The minute we move toward the light switch, she starts to scream. We don't feel comfortable with just letting her cry it out, so we stay in her room until she falls asleep. Meanwhile, she opens her eyes every few minutes to check on us. There have been many times when she seemed completely asleep, but woke up as soon as we got up to leave. What can we do?

A There is a simple, creative way of freeing yourselves from bed-time bondage. First, make a picture story of the things you do to get your daughter ready for bed. Either draw pictures that represent each step of the routine or cut them from magazines. Include a bathtub (for taking a bath), some food (for eating a snack), a toilet, a book (bedtime story), and a bed (for going to sleep). Once you have your pictures, arrange them in order on a strip of poster board and hang this "bedtime poster" somewhere in your daughter's room, where she can see it from her bed (perhaps over her bed). You'll also need a portable kitchen timer.

Tell her that the pictures tell the story of how all children, everywhere, go to bed. You want to convey the idea that bed-time is universal rather than something done only to her. As you begin her bedtime routine, point to the first picture, asking, "What's the first thing mommies and daddies do to help children go to bed?" It will help to get excited about her answer, as in: "That's right! You're so smart! And smart children know how to go to bed!" That may sound ridiculous, but two-year-olds like that kind of stuff.

At every step along the way, take her to the bedtime poster and ask what comes next. When you finish the story, set the timer for five minutes or so, telling her, "This is a bedtime bell. When mommies and daddies finish reading children bedtime stories, they set this bell. When the bell rings, that tells mommies and daddies they have to leave and turn out the lights so children can go to sleep." Again, you create the impression that every child in the world has a bedtime bell. (Note: Creating the impression that a certain practice or rule—whether it relates to bedtime, mealtime, behavior in public places, or whatever—is universal is quite effective with this age child. It makes things less personal and thus reduces the likelihood of resistance.)

After setting the timer, sit next to her and talk quietly about what happened that day. When the bell rings, tuck her in, give her your kisses, and exit. The likelihood is she'll accept bedtime as a matter of fact, but if she still screams, then take turns checking in every five minutes or so. Walk casually into her room, reassure her everything's all right, give her another kiss, and walk casually out, disregarding her protests. This whole operation should take no longer than thirty seconds. Eventually, she'll get the message and go off to sleep. After a couple of weeks, bedtime bondage will be a thing of the past.

Q *Brian, our two-and-a-half-year-old, usually goes to bed at eight-thirty without a fuss and sleeps through the night. My husband's job takes him out of town occasionally. Within the last few months, Brian has had a problem going to bed by himself when his daddy isn't home. Instead of going quietly to sleep, he cries and says he wants to sleep with me. I don't feel right about letting him in our bed because I don't want this to become a habit, but I've given in to him on occasion. My mother and several friends have advised that I let him cry it out. What do you think?*

A I have a hard time with words like "never" and "always." More often than not, they're used to transform generally true statements into complete falsehoods. In this case, the generally true statement is "children belong in their own beds." The complete falsehood is "children should *never* be allowed to sleep with their parents."

In Brian's case, I see no reason why he shouldn't be allowed to sleep with you *when Dad's out of town*. This is not comparable to allowing a child to sleep with both parents on a nightly basis. Brian is seeking additional closeness with you as a way of calming the anxiety he experiences at his father's absence. I assure you that this anxiety is a temporary thing, as is his insistence on sleeping with you during those times. The more reassurance you give him, the easier it will eventually be for him to deal with these interruptions in the family routine.

Q *Our almost-three-year-old will go to bed without much trouble, but in the middle of the night he comes into our room and crawls in between us. If we tell him to go back to his room, he begins to cry, which is not a pleasant sound at three in the morning. More often than not, we're too tired to go through the hassle of taking him back to his room and putting him in his bed. After six months of letting him get in bed with us, how do we put a stop to it without making him cry?*

A With some effort, you can get him to sleep the night in his bed. Or with no effort, you can prevent him from crying in the middle of the night. But you can't have it both ways. If you decide, as you should, that he must stay in his bed all night, he'll cry because you're taking control of a situation he has controlled for nearly six months. During that time, he has acquired the belief that his well-being at night depends on being in bed with you. By making him stay in his bed, you will temporarily disrupt his sense of well-being. Ultimately, however, making him stay in his own bed through the night will provide him great psychological benefit. A child who learns to separate at bedtime will have an easier time with other separation experiences as well. He'll be more trusting of his parents and therefore more confident as he moves toward emancipation.

Begin by telling your son, shortly before bedtime, that he will no longer be allowed to make his "night moves." The conversation might go something like this: "Tonight, Billy, you are going to stay in your bed all night long. If you wake up and come into Mommy and Daddy's bedroom, one of us will walk you back into your bedroom and tuck you in your own bed, where you must stay until morning. This is new, and sometimes children have to cry about new things. Mommy and Daddy will see you in the morning, and everything will be all right."

Then, do exactly as you've said you would. A word of warning: Don't do anything until you are convinced that you no longer want him in your bed at night.

Q *Our thirty-four-month-old goes to bed fairly easily but wants us to leave his bedside light on until he falls asleep. We've tried making Delbert go to sleep with his lamp off, his door open, and the hall light on, but he acts afraid and takes much longer to fall asleep. Nine out of ten times, if he has trouble falling asleep, he'll wake up in the middle of the night and call for us. The obvious solution is to leave his light on, but we're concerned that by catering to his fear in this fashion, we might cause him to develop a habit of needing a light on in order to fall asleep.*

A To begin with, it's unlikely Delbert will develop a debilitating addiction to sleeping with bright lights on just because you let him go to bed with a lamp on when he was almost three. Fears, especially those associated with the dark, are fairly common to this age child. They are a side effect of the otherwise miraculous flowering of imagination. Understandably, the young child is not in complete control of the imaginative process, and sometimes it gets away from him.

One way this age child deals with fears is to form attachments to transitional objects like teddy bears, favorite blankets, and bedside lights. These provide imagined protection against things that go bump in the night. In other words, the child's imagination, which invented the fear, is also capable of inventing a solution to it. By indulging the child's attachment to the transitional object of choice, you're not catering to the fear, you're letting it run its course. Under these easygoing circumstances, the child will not develop fixations, believe me. How many adults do you know who still cuddle with teddy bears? (And so what if some still do?)

On his own, Delbert has come up with a solution to his fear of the dark, a way of controlling it that is more desirable than screaming or demanding to sleep with you. By allowing him his bedside lamp, you will strengthen not his fear but his ingenuity, self-reliance, independence, imagination, creativity, and intelligence, not to mention his courage. Furthermore, he will go to sleep quickly and quietly, a joy for which many parents would turn on every light in the house.

Q *We have two sons, one who just turned three and one who's fifteen months. When the first was a baby, we rocked him to sleep. As he got older, I began lying down with him at bedtime. With the second, I simply put him in his crib, kissed him, and left the room. If he cried longer than ten minutes, I went back in, reassured him, and left. If he continued to cry, I repeated this process every ten minutes until he was asleep. By the time he was six months old, he was going off to sleep without a whimper. The three-year-old, however, still gives us problems at bedtime. Both boys sleep in the same room. I put the baby to bed around eight o'clock. When he's asleep, I go in and lie down with the three-year-old. Depending on when he took his nap, he will fall asleep anywhere between nine and eleven o'clock. If I try to leave his room before he's asleep, he gets out of bed and follows me, crying. What do you recommend?*

A The method you used with your second child works well with children who can't or won't get out of bed. So we need to come up with something new for your three-year-old. Let's see . . . yes, I think . . . by gosh, I have it!

First, establish a regular routine for both naptime and bedtime. Naptime should be the same time every day, shortly after lunch. Simply tell your three-year-old that this is everyone's quiet time, and that as long as he's quiet and stays in his room, he can stay awake and play. Set a timer for an hour and tell him he must remain in his room until the bell rings. If he jumps the bell, direct him back to his quarters. If he falls asleep during the hour (which he eventually will), turn off the timer but don't let him sleep past mid-afternoon. If he doesn't fall asleep, let him out when the bell rings.

Next, establish a set bedtime along with a fixed bedtime routine that starts immediately after you put the baby down. As you leave the room after tucking in your three-year-old, place a necklace of beads (or something similar) over the doorknob. Give him permission to come out of his room for whatever reason. But tell him that when he leaves his room, he must take the beads off the doorknob and give them to you. In this way, he "pays" for the privilege of getting out of bed with bedtime wampum.

The first time he comes out of his room, take the beads, give him whatever he wants (within reason), and put him back to bed. This time, as you leave, don't put the beads on the doorknob. This means he no longer has permission to leave his room. If he breaks the rule, take away an important privilege (going outside, watching television) the next day. Of course, you will need to explain all this to him before you start the procedure. In the final analysis, however, this is something he'll figure out in due time if, and only if, you are consistent.

Q *Our two-year-old started climbing out of his crib several months ago. Since then, we haven't been able to get him to stay in his room at bedtime. We tuck Foxworth in around eight-thirty. Before leaving his room, we tell him in no uncertain terms to stay in his crib and go to sleep. Several minutes later, he appears in the den, grinning from ear to ear and wanting to play. We scold him and put him back in his crib. Several minutes later, it's the same story. This goes on for an hour or more every night. Finally, one of us goes into his room and stays with him until he's asleep. At our pediatrician's suggestion, we left a night-light on and closed Foxworth's door, but he became terribly frightened, and things were worse for several nights thereafter. Do you know of a way to correct this problem?*

A No. Nonetheless, I have an idea, so bear with me. First of all, I sense you've been very patient with Foxworth thus far, which is good, because nothing makes a bedtime problem go downhill faster than yelling and screaming.

Take Foxworth's bedroom door off its hinges and cut it approximately in half, leaving the knob in the lower portion. Then rehang it so that each half swings independently. After tucking Foxworth in at night, leave a night-light on and close the bottom part of his door. Give him permission to play quietly in his room until he's ready to go to sleep. This arrangement might make him a bit angry at first, but it won't scare him. After you leave his room, if he stands at the barricade and howls his displeasure, go back every five minutes or so to reassure him and repeat the rules: "You can play in your room until you're ready to go to sleep, Foxworth, but you can't come out." Given a show of confidence on your part, he should adjust to these new circumstances within a few days. Oh, and by the way, you may as well go ahead and move him into a bed.

Q *We are three families being tyrannized by one small child's sleeping habits. Two-year-old William is a generally sunny little person, but he will not go to sleep peacefully. His parents work second-shift jobs, so William spends his weekday evenings with one set of grandparents one week and the other set of grandparents the next. His parents wake him from his nap in the mid-afternoon to take him to wherever he's spending the night, so he's already cranky when he gets there. When he's put to bed, he begins to scream bloody murder. One grandmother rocks him to sleep, while the other lets him stay up until he falls asleep on the floor with his blanket and bottle. On weeknights, his parents pick him up at midnight and take him home, which begins the bedtime battle all over again. They usually just give up and let him sleep with them. I feel certain that William's bedtime problems can't be solved until we all agree to one approach. The question is, which one?*

A You're absolutely right! Little William's bedtime problems cannot be solved until everyone is on the same track. I'd suggest the following:

- On weekdays, take William to where he's spending the night immediately after lunch and put him down for his nap there.
- His bedtime should be the same regardless of where he sleeps. Likewise, a set bedtime routine should precede the brief tucking-in ceremony. He should definitely not be rocked to sleep, stay up until he's exhausted, or allowed to sleep with anyone. Put him down, tuck him in, and leave the room.
- If he screams, use the five-minute method described previously in this chapter (on page 161). At first, his screaming may go on for a couple of hours, but if everyone handles him the same way, it will gradually diminish.
- Keep him in one place until morning. Moving him at midnight will kill the plan.

- If he wakes up in the middle of the night, which is likely until he gets accustomed to the new way of doing things, use the five-minute method again.

No one will have a good night's sleep until William has made the adjustment to his new routine. In other words, things will definitely get worse before they get better. But if everyone hangs tough, light should appear at the end of the tunnel in a short time. Just keep in mind that it's either stress for a few weeks or stress for who-knows-how-many-more years. Take your pick.

Q *After we put our two-year-old daughter to bed, she picks up her blanket, spreads it out on the floor in front of her door, gets her pillow, and goes to sleep on her new pallet. She is very content and gives us no trouble whatsoever about going to sleep. Should we allow her to continue doing this?*

A Why not? As long as she doesn't come out of her room after you put her to bed, then, as John Lennon put it, "Whatever gets you through the night, it's all right, all right." Two close friends of mine have a four-year-old daughter who has been sleeping on a quilt on the floor in her room ever since she was a year old. Periodically, her parents ask her whether she'd like a bed, or at least a mattress. The answer is always "No." I'll say it again: Where bedtime is concerned, the only thing of real relevance is that the child separate from parents at a reasonable hour. *How* the child accepts that separation is a matter of personality, and—in this case, at least—the child's personality should be allowed free expression.

Q *What's the least disruptive way of moving my two-year-old son, who's been sleeping with me since he was a baby, to his own bed?*

A No doubt about it, a two-year-old who's been sleeping with a parent since infancy will not take kindly to being moved to his own bed, and this age child cannot be persuaded, rewarded, or punished into cooperating. Nonetheless, the move needs to be made, and the sooner the better. Since there is no way of getting over this hump without at least a moderate amount of disruption, the best approach is to just make up your mind and do it. The more determined you are, the sooner it will all be over.

In times like these, I recommend calling on the mystical powers of the "Doctor." With a shrug of your shoulder, tell your son that the Doctor says he has to sleep in his own bed from now on. By invoking a third party, one whose authority the child recognizes, you neatly defuse the otherwise inevitable power struggle.

Put your son in his own bed, read him a story, kiss him goodnight, walk out of the room, and be prepared to take him back, firmly but gently, over and over again. If he just lies there and screams, go back every five minutes or so, reassure him, kiss him, remind him what the Doctor has said, and exit stage left. In two months, the whole process should be over. But if you wait another year, this could take a lot longer. Do it now!

Q *Our twenty-eight-month-old is waking up anywhere from two to five times a night (on a bad night, about every two hours). She comes to our room crying. We simply tell her it's still nighttime and walk her back to her bed. She immediately goes back to bed and back to sleep. Sometimes all we have to do is tell her to go back to bed, and she will put herself back to sleep. We are having difficulty finding the motivation behind this behavior, since she doesn't want us to lie down with her, nor is she angling to get into our bed. Plus, she doesn't fight us when we put her back to bed. She sometimes comes in saying she is scared, but again she will go right back to sleep. We have a new baby, so getting up with both kids is really wearing us out! And* *by the way, this started a couple of months before the baby was born but has since gotten worse.*

A I doubt there's any motivation behind your daughter's behavior at all. What you're describing is a sleep disturbance, pure and simple, not some psychological phenomenon. It is not unusual for a child's sleep patterns to change around age two. The child may begin taking fewer naps, taking longer to fall asleep, or— as with your daughter—waking up periodically during the night. The fact that she says she's scared is probably because at the outset of the problem, you asked, "Are you scared?" If so, then you put the idea in her little head!

In many cases, the explanations children give for their own behavior amount to nothing more than ideas they've picked up from adults. Questions often confuse toddlers. Their best defense, therefore, is to simply agree. In legalese, it's called leading the witness. In this case, your daughter answers that yes, she's scared.

When a toddler wakes up in the night crying, just supply comfort. Do not ask questions. Reassure the child that all is well, that you're taking care of business. Get the child back to sleep as soon as possible, in his or her own bed. When parents bring the child into bed with them or get in the child's bed, the likelihood of continued night waking is greatly increased.

The solution: At her bedtime, stretch a ribbon across the doorway to your daughter's room. Locate it so that she'll run into it (chest height) if she walks out of her room in the middle of the night. Tell her that when she feels the ribbon, she must go back to bed. Rehearse the procedure with her.

Now, this is not going to work magic. Getting it to work is going to take calm, authoritative persistence on your part. When she wakes up and comes into your room, simply take her back to her room and remind her that the ribbon means "get back in bed and go back to sleep." In a week or so, this should be history.

Q *My two-year-old grandson has slept with his parents since*
he was born, but with the birth of a third child (he also has a
four-year-old sister), he moved to a bed of his own in an
adjoining room. Since he refuses to cooperate in the new sleep-
ing arrangements, either my son or daughter-in-law rocks him
to sleep, which might take an hour or more. Then, without fail,
he wakes up in the middle of the night and goes to his parents'
bed, where the new baby is sleeping. The parents try to make
him go back to his bed, but oftentimes, the father goes to the
other room to sleep. At other times, the two-year-old wakes up
his older sister, and then they wake up the entire house.

A Let this be a lesson to all who are reading this. The "family bed"
may seem warm and fuzzy, but it often devolves into chaos of this
sort. If this two-year-old had been trained to sleep in his own
bed since birth, this would not be happening. Assuming no other
behavior problems had developed, he'd be a well-adjusted child
who was perfectly content with a room and a bed of his own.

Despite the claims of family bed advocates, not one study
done by an objective researcher has demonstrated benefit to the
children so bedded. The American Academy of Pediatrics rec-
ommends against the practice, noting that infants are sometimes
smothered by parents who inadvertently roll over on them.

Rarely do I meet a father who has initiated this unnecessary
practice. It's nearly always the mother's call, and the mother in
question is almost invariably one who has bought into the propaganda that bedding with her child promotes so-called attachment or mother–child bonding.

There are no two ways about it. A child who sleeps with
his parents develops a dependency on sleeping with his parents,
one that comes back to haunt all concerned when the parents
decide the child's presence in the bed has become inconvenient.
Meanwhile, this child has been deprived of the inestimable

benefit of learning that he was not a member of the wedding, that the marriage is not a threesome. During my private practice years, I saw a lot of these kids. As a rule, they were not happy campers. In this case, the parents are obviously slow learners, as they're making the same mistake with the newborn.

At this point, about the only solution is for the parents to wait this transition out. In the meantime, they should get the newborn out of their bed and into her own room and make it perfectly clear to the two-year-old that no one is going to sleep in Mommy and Daddy's bed ever again but Mommy and Daddy.

Q *My almost-five- and two-year-old boys recently moved to a bunk bed to be in the same room. I'm delighted that they have a wonderful relationship, but they no longer take their nap without a major struggle. I know that being together in the same room is fairly new and exciting, but they don't have the same problem at bedtime. Do you have any ideas?*

A I have several, in fact. They're all absolutely brilliant, so you take your choice:

- Don't put the kids together for naptime. Put one of them in your bed, for example. However, you may find that if the two-year-old is separated from his older brother at naptime, he may cry, which could cause his brother to become upset. In other words, you might exchange one problem for another.

- Put them in their bedroom, but don't require them to sleep. Just call it quiet time. Close their door, put an alarm clock outside that's set to ring when you're ready for chaos to resume, and tell them they have to stay in the room, playing quietly, until the alarm goes off. They aren't likely to play quietly, however, in which case you'll just have to accept that there is no perfect solution to this problem and ignore them for the duration. Console yourself with the fact that the chaos is at least contained.

- "Deputize" the five-year-old. Tell him that he's responsible for seeing to it that his brother takes a nap. Give the impression that this is a very important responsibility and tie it to a reward of some sort. The problem here is that if he doesn't succeed, he may begin to resent his younger brother, and the relationship will suffer.

- Tell them that if they don't take a nap, they still have to remain in their room for the full naptime, but their bedtime moves ahead one hour. The flaw in this solution is that the older boy will be the only one who understands what that really means, and he may become very frustrated in his attempts to get his brother to cooperate. I think you agree that when all is said and done, it's more important that they continue to have a good relationship than take naps.

If I were in your shoes, I'd take the easy way out: Put them in their room and call it quiet time. But you must decide what works best for your family.

Q *As I write this e-mail, it's 10:00 p.m. and my three-year-old daughter just fell asleep. She used to sleep twelve hours a night, from 7:00 p.m. to 7:00 a.m., but she hasn't done that in months. I tried moving her bedtime to 7:30 p.m. and then to 8:00 p.m., but that didn't help. Every night I take her blankie and sleep doll so she has nothing to play with, but she just lies there and sings and talks to herself. She shares a room with her six-month-old brother and wakes him up repeatedly during the two or three hours it takes for her to fall asleep. We tried spanking, but that didn't faze her, so we stopped. Taking away toys and privileges doesn't work either. The only good news is she doesn't come out of her room. Help!*

A You're fighting a losing battle. You can put a child to bed, and you can enforce staying in the room, if not the bed, but you cannot make the child go to sleep.

You've created a power struggle out of this issue, and it is axiomatic that when parents enter into power struggles with children, problems always get worse. This is an example of what I call parenting physics: Any attempt by parents to force what cannot be forced, to control what cannot be controlled, will result in an equal and opposite reaction.

Accept that you've lost. Only then can you begin to solve the problem. Here's how: First, put your infant to bed in some other area of the home, at least temporarily, even if that means moving his crib into your room. Then, put your daughter to bed when you want her to be in bed. If that's 7:00, so be it.

It's worth mentioning that keeping a child up late in hopes that she will be more tired when she goes to bed increases the chance of the child becoming overtired, and overtired kids have great difficulty falling asleep. Tuck her in, kiss her goodnight, wish her sweet dreams, leave her room, and let her take her sweet time getting to sleep. If you stop fighting with her and just let this issue alone, I predict that within a couple of weeks, maybe three, she will be falling asleep within an hour.

Q *For the last month, our two-year-old son has started waking up around three o'clock in the morning, wide awake. After he finally goes back to sleep, he wakes up for good at 6:30 a.m. Before this started, he slept through the night until 7:00 or 7:30 a.m. His afternoon nap is now a good half-hour shorter as well. I think he's overly tired, and this is why he is waking up during the night. Consequently, I think he needs to go to bed earlier. My husband thinks the opposite and wants to make his bedtime later. Please tell us, who's right?*

A You are. Concerning sleep and youngsters, the general rule is that the later a young child stays up at night, the less well the child will sleep. Being overtired is the biggest cause of sleeplessness and restless sleep in small ones.

Having said that, there is no guarantee that putting your son down earlier in the evening will solve the problem. He may be making a transition in his sleep habits, one that will work itself out in a month or so. Nonetheless, I'd put him to bed no later than 7:30 in the evening, if for no reason other than providing the two of you with more child-free time.

Q *My two-year-old is still sleeping in her crib. When we put her in for a nap, she begins jumping up and down, holding onto the side. (She was also doing this at night, but that has stopped.) We have tried spanking and taking away a favorite activity. Nothing seems to work! We feel like she still needs a nap because she acts tired when she doesn't take one. Please help!*

A This is not a parenting problem; this is a parent problem. The fact that at naptime your daughter takes the opportunity to exercise gross motor skills and have fun at the same time (after all, they are virtually synonymous) is consuming too much of your emotional energy. You will both be candidates for the loony bin by the time she's five.

Simply put her in the crib, leave, and let her do her jumping thing for as long as she likes—she might eventually fall asleep. And if she doesn't, so what? Leave her in there for a couple of hours anyway. If she falls asleep at the ninety-minute mark, leave her alone and put her to bed at her normal bedtime anyway. She will eventually self-adjust as long as you stay on schedule. As it is, it sounds to me as if you're actually preventing this transition from occurring naturally by rushing back in there and threatening and yelling and spanking over something that merits a yawn.

Let the little girl dance!

Q *My just-turned-three-year-old daughter still sleeps in a crib, loves it, and has no interest in sleeping in the big bed in her room. She's a great sleeper, even though her favorite position is all scrunched up at one end. Is there any reason why we should make her move to the big bed?*

A I'm going to assume that the side of the crib is down and that your daughter can get in and out by herself. Indeed, it's a tad unusual for a child this age to still be cribbed, but given that this is her choice and that a big bed is available to her, I don't think this either is a problem. If this were part of a general effort on your part to keep her in an infant state, that would be another story, but this situation doesn't fit that profile. She will make the transition when she feels ready, when she needs more sleeping space, or when her friends begin asking why there's a crib in her room. In the meantime, don't give it a second thought.

CHAPTER

Territoriality and Aggression, or (*Bap!*) "Mine!"

Nothing provokes parent anxiety, panic, anger, guilt, or all of these as much as aggression by toddlers toward other toddlers. This is primarily because of the bogus Freudian notion that parenting produces the child and that everything a child does is directly related to something the child's parents have done (or failed to do, or failed to do properly, and so on). As a consequence, moms are inclined to think that their kids' aggression is a sure sign they've committed some egregious parenting sin. The result is what I call disciplinary paralysis. The mom is so paralyzed that she doesn't respond effectively to her child's aggression because she really doesn't know who needs to be disciplined: her child or her. Under the circumstances, the aggression is very likely to get worse.

With that in mind, let's get one thing straight before we go any further: Aggressive children don't have bad parents, nor is anything *wrong* with them. Most aggressive behavior—no matter how "uncivilized" (biting, for example)—is *normal* with toddlers. As I've said in previous books, most notably *Parenting by the Book* (Howard, 2009), one does not have to teach bad behavior to a toddler. They hit, lie, take and hide other people's belongings (meaning that they covet), and believe they are gods. In other words, they violate nearly every one of the Ten Commandments and seem to be having lots of fun in the process.

A real-life example: An eighteen-month-old child throws himself on the floor and begins screaming and thrashing about because his mother refused him a cookie. Her compassion moves her to pick him up so she can comfort him, and she tells him he can have a cookie after supper, which is imminent. As she lifts him to her shoulder, he hauls off and smacks her across the face as hard as he can. Mind you, this child has never seen or even heard people describe acts of violence of any sort. His parents certainly don't hit each other when they're upset. Where did that come from? It came from his nature. It is a measure of God's mercy and grace that he designed us such that—unlike animals—we do not grow to full size in one or two years. Can you imagine the mother in the above example trying to deal with an enraged toddler who already, at eighteen months, weighs 150 pounds and is as tall as she is?

Not all toddlers are aggressive, mind you, but ones who don't hit or bite do not have better parents than ones who do. Some children are simply more inclined toward aggressive behavior than others. When a toy they're playing with is snatched, some more passively disposed toddlers will sit helplessly and cry. There's nothing wrong with these children because they don't defend their territories. Other toddlers will snatch back and clobber. These aren't *bad* children. There's nothing *wrong* with them, either.

Whether a child is more or less aggressive than the norm is a *temperamental* characteristic. Maybe it's a matter of genetics, but that hasn't been proven. Regardless, it boils down to the fact that they were born that way. That doesn't mean they can't be stopped from hitting or biting, however.

It is possible to stop an aggressive toddler's random outbursts of hitting and biting eventually, but the cure requires that adults be intolerant. Not angry, mind you, because anger will probably make matters worse. They must be calmly but unequivocally intolerant. The fact is, one cannot talk, explain, reason, or even love a toddler out of hurting other children. Those approaches, however well intentioned, are attempts to *persuade* the toddler to stop. It's just not possible to patiently teach alternatives to hurting. Before any teaching can take place, the child must be shown that hurting other children results in consequences he doesn't want to pay. To get through to him, the consequence in question (1) must get his attention (and remember, his attention span is short) and (2) must be delivered with dispassionate intolerance. Anything less won't get through. You probably think I'm talking about spanking. Not really. There's no good evidence that spankings increase aggression, but spanking a toddler is a dicey proposition. With some, spankings make things better. With others, spanking makes things worse. I don't recommend that parents run the risk.

Here's my general anti-aggression formula:

1. Immediately, with no show of emotion, remove the aggressive child from the situation.
2. Communicate, in five words or less, that the hurting, whatever form it took, will not be tolerated, as in, "No hitting!"
3. Separate the child from the group or the activity for at least five minutes. Have him sit in a chair or on the floor during that time. Don't hold him. If he's crying, do not allow him to return to the group until he has stopped.
4. When you return him to the group or situation, get down to his level and say "No hitting" again.

Returning to one of the themes in chapter 3, "Creative Discipline," some toddlers can't be stopped from hurting other children while they are still toddlers. That's why I said earlier that they can be stopped *eventually*. With some toddlers—not many, so don't become despondent—the force needed to stop them from hurting other children would be unreasonable. With a toddler of that very stubborn sort, you will be limited to containing the hurting until he is older. I'll delve more deeply and specifically into that situation in the question-and-answer section at the end of this chapter. Meanwhile, let's take first things first.

Sharing

Toddlers are territorial little people. The space in front of them and everything within it are "mine!" Intrusions into that territory threaten the child's self-concept and therefore provoke distress. The more passive child cries; the more aggressive child strikes out.

Sharing is one of those civilized things, like chewing with one's mouth closed, that parents are in a hurry for children to do. Unfortunately, children are in no equal hurry. Sharing must be taught by parents and teachers who are patient and understand that sharing does not come naturally to the territorial toddler.

Parents can begin planting the seeds of sharing during infancy and toddlerhood by playing the game of "Put-and-Take." Handing an item back and forth between yourself and your infant or young toddler is an early method of teaching the concept of taking turns. As your child grows, you can continue to reinforce this concept by taking turns putting the pieces into a puzzle, or turning the pages of a book, or adding blocks to a tower. You can also create spontaneous teaching situations by offering to exchange things with your child, as in, "I'll share my juice with you. Will you share a cookie with me?"

The ability to share develops in stages: A child first learns to play peacefully alongside other children, then to take turns, then to share without adult prodding. The most one can reasonably expect of two-year-olds, while they are still self-centered and territorial, is what's known as parallel play. During this first step in the socialization process, two or more children will occupy the same general space but will play independently, each doing his or her own thing.

Occasionally, one toddler will raid another's territory, provoking a brief but intense clash of wills. Battles of this sort can be more easily managed by grouping twos according to similarities in temperament. For instance, several passive, easygoing twos can play alongside one another for long periods of time without conflict. On the other hand, a group of active, assertive twos will clash, especially at first, but will arrive at detente within short order if allowed to work things out pretty much on their own. In this instance, the role of the supervising adult is to prevent mayhem, not determine the pecking order.

Expect real trouble when passive toddlers are mixed with active, aggressive ones. The more assertive toddlers, sensing the advantage, will take it. The result: snatching, hitting, and perhaps even biting, all to a chorus of wails from the more passive children.

By age three, children are usually more socially conscious and significantly less self-centered. Reflecting these developments, their play becomes more associative and interactive. Twos play alongside one another, occasionally raiding one another's space, but threes start playing *with* one another, forming their first friendships in the process. For all these reasons, three is the ideal age at which to start a child in nursery school, but even then I don't recommend more than part-time.

Three-year-olds are able to participate in group activities and take turns with play materials, but spontaneous sharing is still a problem for some for whom even learning to take turns continues to be difficult. Helping a three-year-old (or even an older two-year-old) over this hurdle requires no more than a kitchen timer and some firm yet loving direction. Take two children who are playing together but having difficulty with give-and-take over some particularly interesting toy. With kitchen timer in hand, the supervising adult says, "We're going to use this timer to help you learn to take turns with that toy." At that point, set the timer for three minutes, then gradually increase the time as the children get better at the game. Tell them, "Billy, you can play with the toy until the bell rings, then I'll set the timer again, and Robbie can play with it until the bell rings."

This simple technique provides the structure children need to take turns. In most cases, once the toy has alternated hands a few times, the timer will no longer be needed (until the next conflict arises, that is).

By age three-and-a-half or four, if the necessary foundation has been laid properly, a child should be able to share spontaneously and play cooperatively in most settings. However, even the well-prepared child will have occasional problems with letting go of certain possessions, necessitating some adult guidance. Although it may at times be appropriate to insist that a child share, the basic rule when helping children through problems of this sort is to propose solutions that result in neither child feeling like the loser. Above all else, keep in mind that a child's right to ownership of his playthings must be affirmed before he or she will feel comfortable sharing with other children. In advance of a friend coming over, it may be helpful to let a child put away several favorite toys he doesn't want to share. Once he's made his selections, remind him that you expect him to share everything else with the friend. By providing the child with an insurance policy of this sort, you increase the likelihood that the interaction will go smoothly.

Questions?

Q *Two days a week, my two-year-old son attends a Mother's Morning Out program that includes children as young as eight months. At present, he is the oldest child in his class. The problem is that he's hurting some of the babies. Almost every time I pick him up, I get a report of an incident. The teachers have been very patient, but I can tell they're slowly reaching the end of their ropes. The other day, he hit a baby on the forehead with a toy. What should I do?*

A For the following reasons, toddlers and babies should not be grouped together in any sort of day care situation:

- Generally speaking, toddlers don't get it where babies are concerned. They simply don't understand that these little bundles of movement and sound are human beings. No amount of explanation will turn on the light of understanding. A toddler's cognitive (intellectual) skills aren't mature enough to grasp the concept.

- Because they don't get it, toddlers tend to relate to babies as if they are just playthings. In attempts to figure out what babies are, they poke, pinch, bite, and maul (as they tend to do with dogs and cats). And lo and behold, they get fascinating reactions—from the infants and from adults.

- Some toddlers, when reprimanded for something, will stop doing it right away. Others continue doing the something no matter how many times they are reprimanded. You can't predict what's going to happen if you put babies and toddlers together.

- Toddlers don't know their strength and don't understand that the exploring and experimenting they do with babies are often hurtful. To take one example, they don't know that lying across a baby's face shuts off the baby's air supply. In short, the potential risk requires that an adult be always present, if not to prevent hurt (which isn't always possible) then at least to intervene before the hurt becomes life threatening.

The same problem often arises in a family setting. Emergency room physicians and pediatricians will attest that the annual number of infants seriously injured by toddler siblings is not insignificant.

Q *My four-year-old is very aggressive, sometimes even violent, toward his younger brother, age thirty months. I don't think he's completely to blame for their conflicts, but when he gets mad, he sometimes lashes out with a punch or a slap or a kick. A therapist friend of mine told me I need to stay out of it, that ignoring their conflict will facilitate extinction, as he put it. He also said that punishing the four-year-old will only make matters worse. Is there something I can do besides turning a deaf ear?*

A In the first place, ignoring human-on-human violence doesn't facilitate extinction. It enables the behavior. The fact that you don't reward your four-year-old's attacks on his younger brother by paying attention to them is more than outweighed by the fact that his attacks pay off in other ways. He gets the toy, his brother gets out of his way, he feels the addictive surge of dominance, and so on.

You need to put a stop to this, and fast. If the younger sibling were able to hold his own with his older brother, I'd say let them work it out. But you're not describing sibling conflict or rivalry; you're describing sibling abuse. The two-year-old needs your protection, and the four-year-old needs to be stopped. The only way to do that is to punish him. You might have been able to use non-punitive methods successfully when the aggression first started, but at this point attempts to counsel the four-year-old into handling his frustration in a civilized fashion are going to fall flat.

Not only is punishment the answer, but it has to be more powerful—a lot more powerful—than the payoff he's currently experiencing when he hits. I advocate a zero-tolerance policy. When the older child hits, kicks, slaps, or throws something at his brother, don't threaten, remind, or warn. Take him immediately to his room, confine him there for the remainder of the day, and put him to bed right after supper. You should be firm but not angry.

Make sure you keep telling him that the only way he can avoid going to his room is to come to you when his brother is upsetting him. Assure him of your help with whatever is making him mad.

Q *My two-year-old loves her eleven-month-old little sister and usually will play nicely with her. At times, however, she gets excited and becomes rough. She recently bit her three times while playing, and she will also try to wrestle with her while hugging her and laughing. How do I discipline the rough behavior but encourage affection and playfulness?*

A You may well be giving your daughter mixed signals about the roughhousing, acting upset on one occasion and then under-standing and patient on the next. Your two-year-old knows what she is doing, and she knows that she is causing pain to the baby. Therefore, your reaction should be one of stern disapproval, and consistently so. Older sister needs to know exactly how you feel about her rough treatment of her little sister.

My standard recommendation in situations like this, one that has solved the problem for lots and lots of parents, is to keep the older child completely away from the baby for a week. During this time, set a perimeter of about ten feet around the baby and forbid the older child from entering that safe zone. Without communicating anger, make it clear to your toddler that this new rule exists because she hurts the baby when she plays with her. Don't mince words about this.

After a week of quarantine, begin to allow brief, supervised sessions during which the two-year-old can interact with the baby, first touching, then holding, and so on. The week of deprivation causes the older child to want to be with the younger one, and she will figure out what she has to do to accomplish that. Over the next week, gradually allow more and more interaction. If the roughness starts again, go back to square one. My experience is that within a week or two, the problem is solved.

Q *Our seven-year-old son and two-and-a-half-year-old daughter squabble with each other constantly, mostly over taking and playing with each other's toys. The problem is our daughter. She will hit, scream, and throw things when she is angry. She wants to be in her brother's room, doing whatever he is doing, and he doesn't want to keep his door closed. He's not rough with her, but he deliberately aggravates her. We have tried time-outs and separating them. With this sort of age gap, is there some way of stopping the almost constant uproar?*

A Yes, there is. When sibling conflict involves a two-year-old and an older child, any attempt to aim corrective discipline at the toddler is going to fall flat on its face. Holding both children equally responsible for the problem isn't going to work until the younger child is at least three, so until then, the only effective solution is to make the older child *completely* responsible for the problem. That may seem unfair, but the fact is that an older child ought to be able to prevent the problem from happening. In this case, the fact that your son enjoys aggravating his younger sister further justifies holding him responsible.

The solution is obvious and simple: Your son should close and if necessary lock his door. That accomplishes two things: It establishes a physical boundary between him and his sister, and it forces her to begin learning to entertain herself.

Allow one outburst a day. The second outburst means your son's not accepting his responsibility for the problem. As a result, he goes to bed an hour early, and every subsequent outburst shaves an additional thirty minutes off his bedtime. I just bet that will be sufficient motivation for him to keep his door closed.

Q *Is it okay to use time-out with a child who's barely two? While I was watching church nursery today, a two-year-old boy started pushing and hitting the other children. I put him in a chair every time and told him when to get up and not to push and hit, but as soon as he got back up, he went right back to hitting and pushing. Finally, I put him in a crib because the other children were getting very upset, and it seemed the only way to solve the problem was to contain him. Are there better ways to handle this when you don't know how the parents discipline at home, if they discipline at all?*

A Although time-out works with some two-year-olds, it has no effect at all on others. In general, consequence-based discipline does not work reliably with toddlers for the simple reason that their memory is not well developed enough to remember that certain behaviors resulted in certain consequences, or any consequences at all. That's why, like the child in question, a toddler is likely to keep doing the same infuriating things over and over again, even though someone punishes him each and every time. For this reason, discipline methods that work with children three and older do not always work with toddlers.

When a child this age seems impervious to attempts to correct misbehavior, about all one can do is contain the misbehavior behind gates, in cribs, in playpens and so on. That's what you did, and you did fine. Eventually, given consistency on your part, this child will get it.

Q *The park in the center of our neighborhood is full of parents and children of all ages every afternoon. My almost-three-year-old daughter is having a problem with a much smaller two-year-old. Often my daughter will bring along a doll or other toy to play with, but she usually loses interest after a while. At that point, the toddler will start playing with it. Suddenly, my daughter wants it back. If I tell her that she should share, she begins a tantrum, and we have to leave. Last week, she was better about sharing, but when I told the toddler that it was time for her to give the toy back to my daughter, the other mother looked at me like I was evil, so I gathered up my daughter and left. This is creating a lot of tension for me. What do you suggest?*

A It seems to me that this problem can be solved by not allowing your daughter to take a toy to the park. Your daughter hasn't learned to share, and two-year-olds are incapable of sharing, so the solution is to eliminate the source of the problem: the object to be shared. Or let your daughter take a toy to the park on the condition that she takes one for the two-year-old and lets her play with it the entire time.

Q *Our eighteen-month-old son is in a play group with two children of approximately the same age. The problem is, he doesn't protest if one of them takes a toy away from him. Instead, he simply bursts into tears. How can we teach him to hold his own with other children?*

A The territorial instinct is stronger in some children than in others. Therefore, some children are more dominant and aggressive in play groups, whereas others are more passive. The difference is one of temperament and appears to be innate. It appears that your son is on the passive side of the social style continuum, and there's probably not much you can do about that for now. Later, when he's four or five, you can begin giving him guidance in dealing with more assertive children. Always keep in mind, however, that the only person who can do anything about this interpersonal inequity is your son, and he's never going to do anything about it unless *he* sees it as a problem. The fact that it bothers you not only is irrelevant but in the long run can make matters worse. The more your son sees that you are upset when other children take advantage of him, the more he will look to you to level the playing field.

I'd advise that you keep a respectable distance from his relationships with other children. You and other supervising adults can use the kitchen timer technique I describe earlier in this chapter to get the children to take turns, but you'll have to accept that some toy snatching will take place. When he comes to you for comfort, dry his tears and send him back into the fray with words of encouragement. If a certain toy seems to be the focus of lots of conflict, remove it altogether. If a child in the play group becomes physically aggressive toward another (hitting, biting), remove the aggressor from the group until he's calm. Because you're dealing with a mix of passive and aggressive children, you'll have to accept that there will be days when the group atmosphere will be fairly stormy.

Q *Last week, I picked up our twenty-two-month-old son to give him a kiss, whereupon he hauled off and hit me in the face and laughed. I put him down, knelt in front of him and said, "Don't hit your mommy!" He just smiled and hit me again. What did I do wrong?*

A You used the word "don't," one of the more abstract words in the English language. It refers to the absence of a certain action. In other words, when the brain hears something like "Don't climb the fence," it must first register the directive, "climb the fence," and then cancel the order. Much too complicated for a toddler. When this age child hears, "Don't hit your mommy," he actually hears two things: "Don't" and "hit your mommy." "Don't" does not compute. "Hit your mommy" does. Whammo!

Tell a toddler what you want him to do instead of what you *don't* want him to do. Instead of "Don't climb the fence," say "Get down." Sometimes, however, the opposite of the "don't do" is hard to figure out or cumbersome to express. When that's the case, as it is with hitting, just say, "No!" firmly and with a stern look. So, the next time your son rears back to hit you, stop him (if you can) and say, "No!" If you don't intercept the blow in time, take the offending hand firmly in yours and say, "No!" Either way, he'll get the message. Eventually.

Q *Our two-year-old has started hitting us whenever he doesn't like something we've done to him or doesn't get his way. Is it okay to spank him or pop his hand when he hits us? If not, then what should we do? By the way, don't tell us to sit him in time-out, because he won't stay. As soon as one of us sits him down, he pops back up again.*

A First, remember that you're describing behavior that's normal for this age child. Mind you, not all two-year-olds hit, but enough do, and that makes it normal. Hitting results when the flint of an aggressive two-year-old's personality strikes the iron of something frustrating.

No big deal, actually. Remember that twos are uncivilized. They have yet to learn the ins and outs of appropriate social behavior. When frustrated, they go with their first impulse.

If their first impulse is to hurl themselves on the ground and scream bloody murder, then hurl and scream it is. If their first impulse is to hit, then hit it is.

I would not recommend that you spank or pop your son's hand when he hits you. I'm not altogether opposed to an occasional swat to the bottom, but my experience tells me that spankings usually create more problems than they solve at this age. A spanking is likely to enrage an already frustrated child further, setting the proverbial snowball rolling.

Instead, I recommend you use time-out. Wait! I know you said time-out doesn't work, but hear me out. You apparently think time-out works only if the child sits cooperatively until he's told to get up. In that sense, time-out definitely does not work with most twos, who, like your son, won't sit in one place longer than it takes for their parents to straighten up and take a step or two away. However, if you don't make an issue out of how long the child sits, time-out can work quite well with even the most stubborn two-year-old.

The next time your son hits one of you, get down at his level and with a stem look and a firm tone in your voice, say, "No!" Then lead him to the nearest chair and sit him down, saying, "Sit here until I tell you to get up!" Take a quick step back and say, "You can get up." Then turn around and walk away. The trick is to tell him to get up before he does it on his own. In this rather clever way, you prove your point, which is that you can move him, but he can't move you. By responding assertively (but not aggressively) to his hitting, you demonstrate your control over yourself, the situation, and him as well.

If you do that every time he hits you, he should stop altogether in a year or so. I'm just kidding. But seriously, don't expect a miracle. Twos are as persistent as all get-out (whatever that means), so hang in there.

Q *Our almost-three-year-old has recently taken to hitting us—or at least trying to—whenever he's mad at us for not giving him his way. We've tried explaining to him why he shouldn't hit and have suggested other ways of expressing his frustration, but he doesn't listen. His preschool teachers tell us he's well behaved and gets along well with other children. Furthermore, he's never even tried to hit anyone at school. We wonder, therefore, why he's so angry with us. We recently read an article in which a child psychologist recommended against any form of punishment for hitting. Punishment, she said, will cause a child to repress anger and learn that feelings are bad. She recommended that the child be given an inflatable Bozo the Clown that he can beat up on whenever he has angry feelings. Thinking this might help, we bought our son a Bozo, but his hitting has since gone from bad to worse. What should we do now?*

A I never cease to be amazed at the rhetoric certain professionals invent to justify the positions they take on child-rearing issues. Encouraging children to vent their rages on inflatable Bozos is permissiveness at its worst and most absurd. When and how, may I ask, will a child ever learn to tolerate frustration and control his temper if he's never required to do so?

Growing up involves learning self-discipline, as it applies not only to behavior but to emotions as well. Feelings are private, intimate matters, not intended for unrestrained public display. Teaching a child to control the expression of feeling is a far cry from repressing those feelings or teaching him that feelings are bad.

His teachers say that he's generally well behaved and has never tried to hit anyone at preschool, so there's probably no deep psychological reason for his hitting. He hits you because he's angry with you for not giving him his way. Plain and simple. His frustration overwhelms him, his impulses take over, and he lashes out. He doesn't lash out at playmates or teachers because he can't predict their behavior as well as he can predict yours. It's safe for him to lose his temper with you, so he lets it all hang out.

When he loses control, it's your responsibility to control him. That's what parents are for. What does he need to know? That you won't allow him to hit you. How can you get this across? Easy. Don't let him. Surely you can read his behavior well enough to know when he's about to hit. When the attack comes, demonstrate your authority and control by intercepting the blow. Take his hands firmly in your own and tell him that you will not, under any circumstances, allow him to hit you: "You may not hit me, I am not giving you a cookie before supper [or whatever], and you are going to sit in this chair until I tell you to get up." At this age, a child will sit for a couple of minutes but is more likely to cooperate in time-out if you use a kitchen timer to signal when he can get up. So get yourself a kitchen timer, and when you put him in time-out, set it, saying, "You will sit here until the bell rings."

Later, when the iron is no longer hot, you can talk authoritatively to him about his anger. Don't ask him why he's angry, please! Instead, make statements about anger and hitting: "It's okay to get mad when I won't let you do what you want, but it's not okay to hit. You can tell me you're mad, and we'll talk about it. If you don't feel like talking, you can go to your room until you calm down. But I won't let you hit me, and when you try, I'm going to sit you in the chair. Do you understand?"

Meanwhile, give Bozo to a child who'll give him a good home.

Q *We have two daughters, ages thirty-four months and twenty months. At first, the older child seemed to accept her younger sister, and things went well between them. Within the past few months, however, an often intense rivalry has developed. While it's often hard to tell who started something, the older* *child clearly uses her physical superiority to her advantage. When they get into a scrap, it usually involves a toy. The older child knocks the baby down, snatches things away from her, and has even hit her on a couple of occasions. We don't want to be constantly reprimanding the older one, but feel we must do something when these altercations occur. Can you give us some guidelines?*

A It's important that you intervene as little as possible in their altercations. It goes without saying that you have to get involved when the baby is in danger of getting hurt. You might also need to intervene if conflict occurs in inappropriate situations (e.g., when you have guests) or becomes extremely disruptive. But if it doesn't sound like anyone is getting mangled, stay out of it.

When you do get involved, do so in a way that doesn't assign blame to either of the girls. Don't concern yourself with who started it or who did what to whom. Take the toy away, or separate them for a time, or reprimand them both for making such a disturbance, or all of the above, but don't sympathize with one and punish the other. Although it's probably true that your older child is the aggressor, if you fall into the habit of assigning the roles of villain and victim to the children at this time, you will set the stage for never-ending and ever-escalating sibling rivalry.

If you handle their conflicts without assigning blame, then your second daughter will eventually figure out how to solve the problems posed by having an older sibling. Furthermore, time is going to all but eliminate the older child's physical advantage, so she, too, is going to have to find other ways of asserting herself with her younger sister. Have patience.

Day Care Versus Parent Care, or Who's Minding the Store?

Once upon a time, I believed that a toddler, even an infant, could thrive perfectly well in the daytime care of a person or persons other than a parent as long as the care was truly caring. I believed that the single most relevant issue was the *quality* of the day care experience. If the people who provided the care were committed (as opposed to simply punching a clock) and competently trained, and if the day care environment were responsive to the child's need for affection, attention, exploration, and stimulation, then I couldn't see why a tot was any worse off than he or she would be in the full-time care of a responsible parent. I thought there might even be numerous benefits to children, even children of very responsible, loving parents.

I was wrong. For the past twenty years, that has been my position on this issue, but I've changed my mind. The research I did during the writing of this chapter has convinced me that parent care during the first three years of life is clearly in the best interest of a child. The research indicates, as it has for more than two decades, that although day care might not be bad for children, it's not nearly as good as parent care, even when the parent isn't a candidate for Mom or Dad of the Year. This is not the "politically correct" position, however, for two reasons:

- First, parent care is usually equated with mother care. Although it doesn't matter whether the parent providing the care is male or female, or whether two parents manage their schedules so that they split child care responsibilities, many people feel that my remarks are directed at women.

- Second—and for the moment, gender specific—a working mother is generally viewed as more liberated than a mother who opts to provide home care for her children. As a result, a significant number of people view my remarks as downright regressive, tantamount to suggesting that a woman's place is in the home. I will be accused of being criminally unenlightened, and in fact, I already have been. When I first published my mea culpa concerning young children and day care in my syndicated newspaper column in the *Des Moines Register*, an especially silly editorial accused me of setting the cause of women's liberation back twenty-five years. That's how emotional a topic this can be for women.

The fact is, I am as much for having women achieve self-fulfillment as I am for men. I believe that the best parents are self-fulfilled. However, true self-fulfillment is a mature quality. It is not reckless, impulsive, or driven by self-centeredness. A truly self-fulfilled person does not disregard the needs of others or do things at anyone else's expense. In other words, self-fulfillment is not equivalent to self-gratification. In fact, a defining feature of maturity is the ability to postpone self-gratification. If a parent or parents must postpone self-gratification in the form of career advancement in order to provide at-home care for a young child, so be it. More than anything else, children need parents who are able to make mature, responsible decisions.

The "Changing" American Family

Since the 1950s, the American family has been changing, or so the media inform us. This misinformation has created the subliminal impression that some natural, inexorable evolutionary process is behind the steady increase in single-parent and two-income families and that the only problem arising from this process is the failure of society and government to make sufficiently rapid and effective adjustments to the new set of circumstances.

Here's the truth: Since the 1950s, the American family has been in a steady state of decline, precipitated by social experiments and forces that are fundamentally at odds with a state of family health. The ensuing years have made it clear that the traditional American family cannot coexist with the expansionary policies of the social experiments in question.

Here's another undeniable truth: The American family worked better when there was a parent in the home during the day. In past generations, that parent was almost always female, but gender is irrelevant to the purpose of our discussion. That all-but-constant adult presence provided greater family stability, smoother internal transitions, more effective overall time management, better supervision and care of children, and more efficient delegation of responsibilities, not to mention a lower level of stress. The comfortable division of labor between homemaker and breadwinner was more conducive to a sense of partnership, and therefore it tended to support marriage-centeredness. For all these reasons, the American family of previous generations was a more psychologically secure place in which to live and grow up. All this would be mere theory if not for two indisputable facts:

- The divorce rate in the 1950s was much lower than it has been since, and study after study has demonstrated beyond a shadow of a doubt that children fare much better in two-parent homes.

- The mental health of America's kids was much better in the 1950s than it has been since. Some researchers believe that the rate of child and teen depression is ten times higher today than it was then.

These facts fly in the face of assertions from significant numbers of helping professionals that most of us 1950s kids were raised in dysfunctional families lorded over by parents who were abusive in one way or another. All I have to say about that is, "Hogwash."

The neofeminist movement, one of the social experiments in question, convinced significant numbers of women (and men) that there is no incompatibility whatsoever between career pursuit and child rearing. Reading a recent interview with a married professional woman who has two children, ages three years and seven months, I came across the following statement: "I took eight weeks' maternity leave with my first child, six with my second. I could have taken longer, but in my profession, that's not looked upon favorably."

Excuse me? You have children and you put them in day care as quickly as you can (six weeks!) because you might be put on the mommy track if you don't? What are children, anyway? Hobbies? This woman was actually presented as living proof that it doesn't matter whether children are taken care of during the day by parents or total strangers. What matters is that women do it all!

The superwoman of that interview represents a society that's had the wool pulled over its eyes. She embodies the myth that there are no consequences for a child with parents who try to have their cake and eat it, too. In part because personal sacrifice has come to be viewed as just shy of degrading, we have become a nation of families in various states of fragmentation. The priorities of American families have been inverted, everyone's in a perpetual state of hurry, and psychological resources are stretched to the limit. Families that don't fit this description are regarded almost suspiciously.

The American family is *changing*? That's a very antiseptic way of putting it.

Attachment

From day one, parent or parents and child are engaged in an almost constant exchange of sound and movement. This dance forms an emotional attachment that secures the child's trust in the environment. Trusting that the world is a safe, nurturing place, the child can begin the long journey toward emancipation with confidence, moving away from his or her parents and into the world. As he explores and experiments on the environment, the child exercises and strengthens competency skills. I argue that in all but the most extreme cases, there is no one more in tune with the child, and therefore more capable of properly responding to this process, than the child's parents. The good intentions of even the most well-trained day care workers simply do not compare. To this I would add that the only people who can properly help the child make the critical transition from self-centeredness to parent-centeredness during the third year of life are the child's parents.

Since the 1960s, the mental health and early childhood education communities have been engaged in a cover-up concerning these issues. Not wishing to offend anyone, much less appear out of step with the times, developmental psychologists, early childhood educators, and other professionals have acted as if home care and day care workers were fundamentally equivalent. The impression created has been that if parents know what to look for in a day care center, a young child will be as well off in the care of strangers for forty-plus hours a week, fifty weeks a year, as in the care of a parent. That's a myth. It's a myth that serves the needs of day care providers, employers, and some women, but it's a myth, nonetheless.

Here's the truth, the whole truth, and nothing but the truth: Being cared for during one's tender years in one's own home by a responsible, committed parent is distinctly different, both qualitatively and quantitatively, from being cared for in even the best of day care centers. If these are two distinctly different situations, then the outcomes for a child must also be distinctly different. We are naive to think otherwise. Having proposed what is confirmed by research, I am simply convinced that a child's needs are better served in the former situation.

What are the *possible* consequences of placing an infant or toddler in day care? Lacking in caregivers who are adequately tuned to the child, the child may not develop a sufficient sense of trust. Therefore, the environment appears threatening rather than nurturing and inviting. Insecurity prevents the child from moving creatively out into the world. Either the child withdraws, becoming depressed and clingy, or his explorations appear driven and chaotic rather than creative and purposeful. In this regard, it is interesting to note that as the number of infants and toddlers in day care has increased, so has the incidence of childhood depression and behavioral disorders, including attention deficit hyperactivity disorder, which is characterized by driven, chaotic activity.

Whether clingy or driven, the child's ability to develop a fully strengthened complement of competency skills has been compromised. This sets the stage for the eventual development of a host of potential problems—behavioral, emotional, social, and academic.

Is it possible for a young child who is cared for during a significant portion of the day by a person or persons other than a parent to develop a positive perception of the environment and therefore a positive self-image? Possible, yes, but parents are throwing the dice whenever they entrust the day care of an infant or toddler to someone other than themselves. The first three years of life constitute the single most critical, precedent-setting developmental period. Having parents who are first, available, and second, properly responsive to the child's needs during this time is of utmost importance to the child's developmental integrity. During the first two years of life, it is essential that the child be the center of his or her caregivers' attention. Without this confirmation of self-importance, the child will experience insecurity that, in turn, will delay the emergence of creative behavior. Not only is it logistically impossible for day care workers to place any one infant at the center of their attention, but consider also that day care workers, despite generally sterling intentions, are not emotionally invested in the development of the children in their care. (This does not mean they don't *care*, however.)

During the third year of life—the year during which, remember, the most significant transition in the parent–child relationship is supposed to take place—it is equally essential that the child be slowly but surely guided toward the understanding that he or she is not the center of the universe. The only people who can properly guide the child through this upheaval are people in whom the child has invested tremendous trust. But sufficient trust develops only if the child has been the center of attention during infancy and early toddlerhood. Again, regardless of the level of their commitment, day care workers just don't fill the bill.

Would some children be better off in the care of someone other than a parent? Definitely, but if you are reading this book, then you are not one of those parents. Those parents don't read books like this. You are concerned, committed to doing the best job you can at raising your child, responsible, and caring. And yes, you are also flawed. Even the most responsible, caring parent will make mistakes, become frustrated, and lose patience. But despite your faults and your mistakes, you will do a far better job than someone who does not share your emotional commitment to your child, and your child alone.

Babysitters, Family Home Care, and Other Such Things

Am I saying that infants and toddlers should never be left in the care of third parties? Absolutely not! I am referring here to full-time day care only. I do not mean to include babysitters, Mother's Morning Out programs, or even three-mornings-a-week nursery schools (or whatever they call themselves) in this critique. In fact, I am all in favor of parents making time for themselves and especially their marriages. And I am all in favor of infants and toddlers having experience with adult caregivers other than their parents. But in good conscience, I cannot endorse putting a child of tender years in full-time—as in six to nine hours a day, five days a week—day care.

Where does this leave the single parent who has no choice other than to hold down a full-time job, you might ask. Why, it leaves her having to put her child or children in full-time third-party care. (I am using gender-specific pronouns because although the number of single fathers with custody is increasing, the number of single mothers with custody is still significantly higher.) In that event, she should find the very best circumstances her day care dollar can provide. The next best alternative to parent care is a family home setting in which the caregiver is looking after no more than three children. In that regard, however, a 2010 study found that children in family home day care watch significantly more television than do children in day care centers. So if you're thinking of putting your child in a family home setting, make sure the caregiver is not using television to relieve herself of responsibility for true *care*. Otherwise, a small-scale home setting increases the likelihood that each child will receive sufficient individual attention, and because there is no rotation or staff turnover in a home setting, the infant or toddler can form a more secure relationship with the caregiver. Fewer children also means the caregiver can be more accommodating with respect to variances in sleep, feeding, and activity schedules. A home setting will also feel more familiar and less intimidating to the young child. All this makes for a smoother and less stressful transition.

Within a home setting, the parent usually enjoys greater access to, and better communication with, the actual caregiver. Also, the caregiver in a home setting can be more responsive to the parent's preferences concerning such things as the child's diet, nap schedule, and so on, than is generally possible in a larger group setting.

Since most states now inspect and certify day care homes, the first question to ask a prospective home caregiver is, "Are you licensed?" Although a license doesn't necessarily mean better care, it at least guarantees that the home meets minimum standards.

Group Care Guidelines

If the parent of an infant or toddler has no choice other than group care, then the following considerations are important:

- **Child/staff ratio.** The fewer children there are per full-time staff person, the more likely it is that each child will receive a more sufficient share of individual attention. For toddlers, I recommend that the child/staff ratio be no more than four children per full-time staff person. Unfortunately, many day care centers, especially those that are part of national chains, cannot afford to operate with a ratio this low—another rationale for family home care.

- **Rotation and turnover.** Consistency of care gives the young child more opportunity to form a secure caregiver attachment. Do staff persons rotate in and out of the toddler room during the day? How long has the present toddler care staff been at the center? The answers to these questions give some indication as to the quality of the work environment, the level of employee satisfaction (keep in mind that if employees are unhappy, they aren't going to provide a positive emotional environment for children), the level of staff commitment, and the overall stability of the environment.

- **Experience and training.** How and where have staff persons been trained? What certificates do they hold? Is their education ongoing? How much experience does each staff person have working exclusively with toddlers? What is entry-level pay for a full-time teacher? The answers to these questions will tell you whether day care is a career or just another job.

- **Environment.** The toddler room should be bright and airy, with a neutral odor. There should be plenty of open floor space, as opposed to clutter, and there should be absolutely no playpens. The term itself is a misnomer, since these confined spaces are nothing more than holding tanks that restrict exploration and hence the emergence of essential developmental skills. They should be called boring-pens. The play area should be stocked with simple play materials such as large blocks, dolls, and books. Overall, the room should invite exploration and discovery. There should be dress-up clothes that invite children to play pretend games and stretch their imaginations. In addition, there should be areas for water-play, rest, looking at books, and coloring and working with clay. There should also be an outdoor play area where children can run, jump, climb, swing, and ride push-tricycles—all in the name of developing good motor coordination and a healthy appetite.

- **Attitude and disciplinary style of staff.** Teachers are active, involved, and responsive, as opposed to just standing around. They look relaxed yet on their toes. In general, they look like they enjoy their job and love working with children. When discipline is needed, the staff responds firmly yet lovingly. They are attentive enough to ward off the majority of problems. When a child becomes frustrated, aggressive, or disruptive, they separate the child and remain with him, speaking softly, until he's calm.

- **Parent–caregiver interaction.** One of the neglected aspects of putting an infant or toddler in day care is the risk it poses to the parent's sense of confidence and self-esteem. For example, if a mother feels the new caregiver is having better success with her child, she may begin feeling unsure of herself. If she feels she's abandoned her child, she may become ridden with guilt. In either case, the mother's anxiety will translate into her interaction with her child and set the stage for some potentially serious problems. In a good day care setting, the staff is sensitive to any adjustment problems the parent or parents may be having and will provide the understanding and support necessary to help them through the transition. In the final analysis, the interaction between parent and caregiver is every bit as important as the interaction between caregiver and toddler. When shopping for day care, you should trust your instincts and first impressions concerning the director and staff. Did you get a good feeling from them? Did they seem genuine? Did you like them? Did they seem warm and personable as opposed to "all business"?

Emancipation Is a Two-Way Street

If you are reading carefully, you realize by now that in coming down in favor of parent care during the first three years of life, I am not describing a model for overprotection or smothering. Quite the contrary, the parent who stays at home during his or her child's first three years of life provides a stable sense of trust and promotes greater independence. The secure child is able to emancipate much more quickly and successfully than the insecure child. By investing this time during the child's infancy and toddlerhood, the stay-at-home parent fosters self-sufficiency. The payoff comes around age three in the form of a child who is able to occupy himself for long periods of time, is not demanding or whiny, and is generally able to separate from his parents with ease. In the final analysis, therefore, this is a model for the successful emancipation of both parent *and* child.

With or For?

After I gave a talk in Omaha, a woman approached me and asked what I thought about her decision to stay home with her children, as her mother had done. I took a bold chance and said, "I don't believe your mother stayed home *with* you."

She visibly bristled and shot back, "She did too! What do you know?"

"I know that if your mother was anything like my mother," I answered, "and anything like the dozens of other mothers I came to know during my childhood, she got you fed and dressed in the morning and sent you outside to play, perhaps even with instructions not to come home until lunch unless you had an emergency."

Her eyes widened, her body language relaxed, and her mouth dropped open in amazement. She said, "Well, come to think of it, that's exactly what she did."

"Right!" I said. "Then she wasn't at home *with* you, she was home *for* you, and there is a world of difference. Your mother expected you to be as independent of her as she was of you. She didn't hover over you during the day, finding things for you to do, driving you from one activity to another, making sure you were busy. She didn't measure her adequacy in terms of how much she did for her children. When it came to her relationship with her children, she was a very liberated woman, for sure."

She pondered this for a moment, then said, "So what you're saying is, if I choose to stay home, I must take just as good care of myself as I do my children."

Exactly, and more. I'm saying these supposedly unliberated women were our mothers only when we needed mothers. The rest of the time they were adult women, doing as they chose.

They were not at our beck and call, nor did they think the measure of a woman was how much she did for her children. They expected us to be independent, fight our own battles, occupy our own time, stand on our own two feet. They called themselves not stay-at-home moms but housewives, referring to themselves as women whose primary relationships were with other adults, not children. The exceptions were privately labeled as overly protective and smothering by their peers.

Women of that generation either bristle or laugh when I ask whether, in retrospect, they think of themselves as victims. They insist they were committed. They viewed their work as essential to the conservation of both family and culture. And, I dare say, in the way they lived their lives, they demonstrated that it's possible to be liberated and not work outside the home.

The disingenuous attempt to discredit these women as role models is part of a larger attempt on the part of the self-appointed avant-garde to replace traditional values with nouveau values—ones that endure with others spun from the whole cloth of rhetoric. If it succeeds, the sound we hear will be that of our foremothers turning over in their graves.

Despite rhetoric to the contrary, the American family *worked* as well as could reasonably be expected when husbands were breadwinners and wives stayed home with the children. (It goes without saying that I'm speaking in general terms here.) Once upon a time, this was regarded as simply a logical and necessary division of responsibilities. Unfortunately, over time, this tradition gave rise to stereotypes that debased the general capabilities of women. We began to confuse what women had and had not done with what they were and were not capable of doing. This confusion pumped adrenaline into the neofeminist movement and provided an ideal opportunity for the movement to broaden its power base by convincing American women they were members of a victim class. According to the new feminist manifesto, a woman was not complete, and therefore not liberated, if she relegated herself to the role of housewife. Thus began the cultural devaluing of the traditional female role of full-time wife and mother.

As women were seduced and intimidated by this insidious anti-family agenda into putting their children in day care and entering the work force, the American family went into a precipitous state of decline. In the official language, the American family has simply been "changing" over the last thirty years. This is nothing but a euphemistic way of saying that for at least three decades, the American family has been in a steady state of decline, getting progressively weaker and weaker. And as the family goes, so goes the culture. In the final analysis, America is only as strong as its families are healthy. Restoring our domestic health, therefore, has less to do with raising or lowering taxes to create or eliminate this or that government program, and more to do with a reaffirmation of the traditional family values that were the backbone of this country since its inception. This is the stuff of the culture wars in which we are currently engaged.

Be advised that my interpretation of recent historical processes does not carry with it the recommendation that mothers should stay at home with their children while their husbands go to work. I am thoroughly convinced that a committed stay-at-home father is as capable of providing a properly responsive emotional environment for a young child as a committed mother. Bonding studies have focused almost exclusively on the mother's role, but we are beginning to discover how important fathers are to their children's overall well-being. For example, there is indication that children whose fathers are actively involved in their care are more outgoing and possess generally better social skills and are more accepting of challenges than children whose fathers are less involved. In short, there is every reason to believe that infants and toddlers thrive well when their primary care is provided by loving fathers. The best of all possible worlds, of course, is one in which Mom and Dad share parenting responsibilities as equally as possible.

Questions?

Q *At what age do you think children should start going to pre-school? My son is going on three, and he is home with me. I plan to send him to preschool next fall. Almost everyone I know with children this age began sending their kids to preschool this past September. My friends seem to think my son is missing out on essential developmental opportunities and experiences. I thought it was more important for him to be home with me because this time in his life will be over before we know it. Thoughts?*

A I'm all for children being at home with a parent until at least age three. Furthermore, I remain unconvinced about the long-term value of preschool. Researchers have failed to find any long-term social benefit to preschool and have even discovered that kids in preschool are more aggressive and oppositional than kids who stay at home. A trained observer, watching a group of seven-year-olds at play, would not be able to tell which ones attended preschool and which did not.

No long-term academic benefit has been found, either. Everything else being equal, by the second or third grade, children who attend preschool are indistinguishable from those who did not. The so-called jump-start doesn't seem to last more than a couple of years.

It looks as if the most valid reason for a mother to put a child in a preschool program may be that she needs some time away from him, and he needs time away from her. And those are valid reasons enough.

Q *My well-mannered, easygoing, very loving two-year-old is having trouble at Mother's Morning Out. Last year, he cried every day I dropped him off but would stop within a few minutes. This year, instead of my walking in, we use the carpool line so I don't have to get his brand new little brother out of his car seat. When the supervising teacher tries to get him out of the car, he cries, falls to the floorboard, and struggles. This morning, he actually growled at the teacher as she tried to unbuckle him. Now I'm getting reports he has become defiant and disrespectful in class. Yesterday, he began throwing things after the teacher reprimanded him. She thinks he's insecure because there's a second child in the family, but he doesn't act insecure at home. She's also thinking of doing a special reward system for him, which I think is a bad idea. Do you have any suggestions?*

A I don't think this behavior has anything to do with his younger brother's arrival. This problem started before his brother was born and has simply escalated. I also agree that a special reward system is a bad idea. When a child this age behaves badly, punishment is the answer.

Unfortunately, preschools cannot receive certain accreditations if they punish bad behavior. So take him out of the program. It's not worth the aggravation of keeping him there, especially if the teachers aren't able to do anything truly effective when he misbehaves. Let several weeks go by and then find another program or a smaller, cooperative play group. A change of venue may make all the difference.

Q *Our first child is twenty months old. Two months ago, I went back to work and put her in a church day care center. At first, Stephanie had difficulty separating from me. After a couple of weeks, the crying and clinging stopped, but now I'm more concerned than ever. In the morning, she tells me she doesn't want to go to the center. I'm very direct in telling her that she must go, but I always reassure her of my return. When we arrive at the center, she goes quietly into her classroom. When I come to take her home, however, she gets upset and tells me she wants to stay. When I pick her up, she begins to cry and doesn't usually calm down until we get home. Her teachers tell me it takes her a little time to get into the swing of things, but once she's over the hump, she seems to enjoy being with the other children. What could be going on here, and how should I handle it?*

A My best guess is that Stephanie is trying to tell you, in the only way she can, that she needs more stability. She tells you in the morning that she doesn't want to go to day care. In other words, she prefers the stability and security of home. But she accepts your direction and separates from you without protest. Then, just about the time she's managed, as you put it, to get over the hump and into the full swing of things at the center, you show up to take her home. She protests, you take her home, she makes that transition; the next day, the cycle starts all over again.

You already know that I feel Stephanie is a little young to be in full-time group care, but if your decision to return to work at this time is firm, then I suggest you look into day care arrangements that wouldn't require such dramatic transitions. You might look into having someone come into your home to care for Stephanie. This type of care is generally more expensive than the other options, but as with any other product or service, you get what you pay for. An in-home provider would be able to give Stephanie the individual attention she needs at this stage of her development, and Stephanie wouldn't have to shift gears twice a day. In this context, you might have Stephanie spend one or two mornings a week at a Mother's Morning Out program or toddler play group so she has some opportunity for interaction with other children.

If in-home care isn't affordable or feasible, then my next suggestion would be that you try to find a family home day care setting for Stephanie. The relative familiarity of a home environment might be more compatible with her emotional needs at this point. You'd probably experience fewer problems if you waited to put her into group care until she was at least three.

Q *I've just returned from another disastrous morning at a three-morning-a-week preschool class I attend with my twenty-eight-month-old son. The program is organized around learning experiences designed to stimulate intelligence, imagination, and other developmental skills. While the other children sit calmly paying attention to the teacher, I chase my child, trying to keep him under control. The class only lasts an hour, but when it's over, I'm ready for a nap. How can I get him to mind me during this time?*

A For the life of me, I don't understand why you're attending a pre-school program *with* your son. If the purpose is to teach you how to teach your child, I can assure you that twenty-eight-month-old children don't need teaching. They need environments that encourage exploration and experimentation, and parents who read to them a lot, play with them a little, and supervise them well. A preschool child's imagination and intellect will grow to full capacity without being artificially stimulated with contrived learning experiences.

Besides, don't you need a break? At this age, a part-time pre-school program serves only two purposes: giving the child some social experience and giving the front-line parent some time away from the child. In this type of program, a child begins to learn how to play constructively with other children and how to be independent of Mommy. I encourage you to enroll him in a morning program that accomplishes both goals. I suspect you're paying a lot of money for a program that's more "show" than "go."

Q *I've always heard the most important thing working parents can give their children is quality time. My husband and I both work full-time (I went back to work four months ago), and our almost-three-year-old spends the day in an excellent, church-operated child development center where, because of the support of the congregation, the child/staff ratio is lower than at any other program in the city. After we get home, change clothes, and have dinner, there isn't a lot of time left before our daughter's bedtime. What's the best way to bring quality into the little time we have together in the evening?*

A In the first place, the most important thing two working parents can give their children is a strong marriage. I'm not saying quality time spent with your child isn't important; I'm saying it's more important that you spend quality time with one another.

Keep in mind that, at this age, you should be focused on moving your daughter out of the center of attention in your family and positioning yourselves at the center of her attention.

If, five out of seven days a week, you only have three hours in which to be a family, that's all the more reason for you to keep your family priorities in order during that time. To be sure, a child needs attention from parents, and the younger the child, the more attention is needed. But parents also need time together as husband and wife, and children need to see their parents spending this time together. A child cannot learn that her parents' marriage is the keystone relationship in the family if, whenever they're together as a family, they act almost exclusively from within the roles of mother and father.

Furthermore, by now you should expect your daughter to be more responsible for keeping herself occupied. By the time a child is three, she should be able to play independently for most of the evening, making only occasional requests of her parents. Parents, on the other hand, are responsible for encouraging that independence by providing her with creative playthings, giving her guidance as needed, reinforcing her accomplishments, and occasionally playing with her, but not to the extent that they become her playmates.

As your daughter's bedtime approaches, it makes good sense to spend time preparing her for this transition. A period of closeness during which you bathe her, read to her, and talk quietly to her for a few minutes before tucking her in and leaving her room is definitely needed, but evening after entire evening of two-on-one will prevent the transition to parent-centeredness that is so critical at this stage. Naturally, the weekends will find you spending more time with her, simply because there is more time to spend. Nonetheless, you still need to find plenty of opportunity for marriage-time.

Q *We are teachers of two-year-olds in a child development center. At this writing, the ten children in our group range from twenty-six to thirty-two months. Our problem is Randolph, a sweet and loving thirty-month-old who will not join group activities and generally goes limp when we tell him to do something like pick up toys. He's not shy, because he's very social in free play situations where there's little, if any, structure. When we have an organized activity, however, he will usually move to another area of the classroom and do his own thing. If we coax, he ignores us. If we try to physically make him join the group, he becomes a wet dishrag. Mind you, he's not disruptive, just uncooperative. We've tried everything except ignoring him, which is impossible because we don't want the other children thinking they have permission to follow suit. We also feel an obligation to make sure Randolph benefits from being in the program, not to mention that his parents get their money's worth. Do you have any suggestions?*

A I understand your reluctance to ignore Randolph, but if you've pulled out all the stops and nothing has worked, then perhaps ignoring is all you can do. But don't despair! In the long run, ignoring just may turn out to be the most strategic of all approaches.

As I've said before, it's difficult to *correct* the behavior of a child this age. First, two-year-olds do not readily make the connection between misbehavior and consequences. As a result, even the most well-thought-out punishment may have no lasting impact at all. Furthermore, as anyone who's ever tried to get a two-year-old to sit in a chair knows, the attempt to enforce consequences may only create more problems than it solves. Finally, this age child has yet to acquire a highly coveted set of privileges, so disciplinary leverage is lacking. For all these reasons, it's generally more realistic to think in terms of *containment* than *correction* when disciplining a two-year-old.

I suspect Randolph is feeding off the attention you've been giving these problems. By ignoring him when he separates himself from the group, by letting him do his own thing, you not only contain the problem to Randolph but also starve it of fuel. If he's not successful at getting your attention, he may eventually run out of gas.

How do you explain this to the other children? If they ask, simply tell them, "Randolph isn't going to join us, so we're going to read [or whatever] without him." If another child tries to join him, just be firm and unequivocal in bringing him back to the group. In other words, you don't need to give an elaborate explanation or justification. You say so. That's all any other child needs to hear.

Concerning your obligations to Randolph and his parents, fear not! I can assure you Randolph is benefiting from the program regardless of the level of his participation. In any case, he will get from the program what he's ready to get and no more. Remember, you can't push a river.

Q *We are the grandparents of a very sweet but spoiled thirty-month-old whose parents recently won a week's vacation in Tahiti. They asked us to sit while they're away, which we're delighted to do. After we agreed, however, conditions began creeping into the discussion. We'd like to take him with us on an adventure of sorts, but they don't want him away from home except for day trips. They are concerned he will suffer some sort of psychological trauma if he's separated not only from them but from his security environment (as they put it) as well. We discovered that he's never been left with anyone, not even for a few hours, and that his parents lie down with him every night until he's asleep. (They say they're only going to do this until he's older and more secure.) Do you have any advice for us?*

A This is exactly the sort of thing parents of this generation have been conditioned to agonize over. Granted, your grandson's parents seem to be agonizing a bit more than most, but this hypersensitivity to the imagined emotional frailty of children is typical of today's parents, the first generation to believe that psychologists and other supposed experts (like yours truly!) know more about raising children than do grandparents.

In truth, human children are extremely resilient. If a thirty-month-old is basically secure, then being left in the care of a familiar and competent person—grandparent or otherwise—for a week is not going to be disruptive. Furthermore, whether or not the child is in his security environment during this time is immaterial.

Keep in mind, however, that in this case we may not be talking about an entirely secure child. Sleeping with (even lying down with) a two-year-old does *not* promote security. Nor does never leaving the child in the care of others. In both cases, the separation issue is being avoided. This age child cannot feel a complete sense of security unless his parents have given him permission to stand on his own, venture away from them, experience autonomy, be his own person. To do that—to be given permission to grow up—the child must know it's okay to be separated from his parents. He must know that when they go away, they always come back.

Avoiding separation hobbles the growth of autonomy and promotes insecurity. Furthermore, the longer one waits to confront and resolve this critical developmental issue, the more difficult and painful it will be for all concerned. This situation provides an ideal opportunity for starting down the road to resolution. For the sake of a smooth transition, you should arrive at the parents' home one or two days before their departure. During that time, it should be business as usual. No mention should be made of the fact the parents are leaving. A buildup of any sort will simply sensitize your grandson that something is about to happen that's making his parents act very different. His parents' uncomfortable behavior will increase the likelihood of clinging and screaming when the moment for goodbye arrives.

On the morning of his parents' departure, say, "Guess what? You're going in the car with Grandma and Grandpa today!" After he's dressed and his parents say their (very brief) good-byes, put him in the car and off you go! Later, when he asks questions about his parents, you answer them simply, honestly, and matter-of-factly. When he asks you to lie down with him at night, do what your common sense tells you is right. In the final analysis, it's his parents' job to resolve that issue, not yours. And I'd advise them not to waste a night in resolving it once they return from Tahiti.

CHAPTER

A Final Word or Two

The worst of times, the best of times. That description fits no other stage of human growth and development as well as it does toddler-hood. Sometimes terrible, but always lovable, the toddler careens through this eighteen or so months of life in constant search of answers to "What is it?" and "How does it work?" The compelling nature of these questions spells lots of work for parents. The trick is to find the line between allowing the child the freedom to discover what makes the world tick and keeping the child from getting into trouble. He needs the freedom to begin discovering who he is and who he can become, and at same time, learning that parents are in charge. And a fine line it is. That means, dear reader–parent, you are going to make mistakes. You are going to lose your patience, over-react, underreact, and fail to react until far too late. You are not a perfect being; therefore, you will never be a perfect parent. You won't even get close. Bad news, eh?

Ah, but the good news is that children are extremely resilient, usually much more so than their parents. It follows that children gen-erally recover from their parents' mistakes far more quickly than their parents recover from the anxiety and guilt of making them. Have you ever noticed how forgiving little children are? They seem to realize that their parents' mistakes are nothing more than a consequence of being human, slightly amplified by the tendency to take children much too seriously, and that their parents have great difficulty forgiving themselves. So just when you can't feel any worse about some parenting crime you committed, your little one crawls up on your lap and snuggles in for a hug, as if to say, "There, there, now everything's still all right in my life, so take it easy on yourself, okay?"

And the further good news is that if you've taken the time to read this book, you're not the type of parent who's likely to make the same mistakes over and over again. You're going to learn from them, and as time passes, you're going to become a better and better parent. You'll never be perfect, but you'll always be the only mother or father your child will ever want. So take that as a vote of confidence and do your best, because your best is always and forever going to be good enough.

Enjoy!

INDEX

Family psychologist John Rosemond is director of the Center for Affirmative Parenting, headquartered in Gastonia, North Carolina. CAP is a national resource center that provides parents with practical parenting advice and materials. Toward that end, CAP conducts workshops and educational presentations for parents and professionals who work with children. CAP also has available print, audio, and audiovisual materials on parenting and child development.

Since 1978, John has written a nationally syndicated family column that currently appears in more than one hundred newspapers across the United States and Canada. His columns have appeared regularly in *Better Homes and Gardens* magazine and *Hemispheres,* United Airlines's` in-flight magazine.

Throughout the year, John is in demand as a public speaker. His humorous, provocative parenting presentations and workshops have drawn consistently high marks from parent and professional groups all over the country.

Last, but by no means least, John is husband to Willie and father to Eric and Amy, both of whom are married with, between them, seven children. Eric is a corporate pilot. Amy is a homemaker.

Those interested in obtaining information about John's presentations, workshops, or parenting materials can do so by going to his Web site at www.rosemond.com.